S0-BIM-755

Intimations of Divinity

American University Studies

Series V
Philosophy

Vol. 72

PETER LANG
New York • Bern • Frankfurt am Main • Paris

David Platt

Intimations of Divinity

PETER LANG
New York • Bern • Frankfurt am Main • Paris

Library of Congress Cataloging-in-Publication Data

Platt, David
Intimations of divinity / David Platt.
p. cm.—(American university studies. Series V, Philosophy ; vol. 72)
1. God—Proof. 2. God—Knowableness. 3. God—Proof, Empirical. I. Title. II. Series.
BT102.P57 1989 212—dc19 88-21726
ISBN 0-8204-0856-5 CIP
ISSN 0739-6392

CIP–Titelaufnahme der Deutschen Bibliothek

Platt, David:
Intimations of divinity / David Platt. – New York; Bern; Frankfurt am Main; Paris: Lang, 1988.
(American University Studies: Ser. 5, Philosophy; Vol. 72)
ISBN 0-8204-0856-5

NE: American University Studies / 05

Printed by Weihert-Druck GmbH, Darmstadt, West Germany

TABLE OF CONTENTS

ACKNOWLEDGEMENTS

I wish to thank the following: Dean Patricia Cormier, Wilson College, and Wilson College's Paul Swain Havens Memorial Fund for support for this project; Professors Raymond Anderson and W. Norris Clarke, S. J. for their reading of the manuscript and their many valuable suggestions; Nancy Augustine for path-smoothing and technical advice; Helen Cumley for word-processing and problem-solving; Janice Fetters for accurate typing; Barb Batz and Candy Boettcher for willing, cheerful aid; Susan Jordan for making the laser printer available and Deb Bumbaugh for help in using it; Hillary Wasserman, Production Editor at Peter Lang, for prompt responses and much advice. I cannot express my thanks sufficiently to my wife, Helen, not only for her editorial assistance but just for being there and being herself.

Thanks go also to the following for their kind permission to use copyrighted material:

<u>International Philosophical Quarterly</u> for "God: From Experience to Inference: A Phenomenological Study." Vol. X, No. 4, Dec. 1970, pp. 598-610; "The Seashore As Dwelling in the Fourfold: An Ontic Explication of Heidegger." Vol. XXV, No.2, June 1985, pp. 173-184; "Divinity as a Given." Vol. XXVII, No. 4, December 1987, pp. 381-392.

<u>Journal of the American Academy of Religion</u> for "Some Perplexities Concerning God's Existence." Vol. XXXIV, July 1966, pp. 244-252; "Things, Persons and God: A Phenomeno-

logical Contrast." Vol. XXXVI, No. 4, December 1968, pp. 366-372.

Kluwer Academic Publishers for "Is Empirical Theology Adequate?" in International Journal for Philosophy of Religion, Vol II, No. 1, Spring 1971, pp. 28-42.

Random House for a citation from Hume's "Dialogues Concerning Natural Religion" in The English Philosophers From Bacon to Mill, ed., E. A. Burtt, 1939, p. 751.

Unwin and Hyman for a citation from J. N. Findlay, The Discipline of the Cave, 1966, p. 157.

INTRODUCTION

THE EMPIRICIST APPROACH TO RELIGION THROUGH PHENOMENOLOGICAL ANALYSIS

In recent years empirical theism has fallen on hard times. Natural theology, while practiced within the Catholic tradition, has not been a major force in Protestant circles. Within the confines of the philosophical community, when religious discourse has not been dismissed outright as meaningless, it has been analyzed in terms of what sometimes is referred to as "God talk." While some of this philosophy of religion within the analytic tradition has been profound, some of it has been carried on as a linguistic game coupled with the attitude that it is somewhat improper to talk in a _substantive_ manner about the great issues of God, freedom and immortality. Some of the great themes such as freedom, suffering, death and human anxiety are well treated within the phenomenological and existentialist traditions. I should like to turn explicitly to the question of the divine component in experience which is often a peripheral concern to existentialists whose interests seem mainly geared to the human condition.

Empirical approaches to theism suffered a severe blow with Hume's acute criticism of the argument from design in the "Dialogues." In more recent times, liberal Protestantism has put more emphasis on the "social gospel" than on the God question as such. In reaction Barthian neo-orthodoxy reverted to the God question but dealt with it exclusively in terms of revealed doctrine. The issue of revelation is an important one, but does not lend itself to treatment in a purely philosophical context. To appeal to revelation may make religious good sense, but it is to put oneself out of bounds as far as philosophical treatment is concerned. From a philosophical perspective one can approach theism in either an a priori or an empirical manner. The standard a priori approach is found in the famed ontological argument, stemming from St. Anselm in the eleventh century and extending to Hartshorne and others in our own time. Attempts to prove God's existence a priori through the ontological proof are remarkably unpersuasive. As one dedicated to a liberal empiricism I used to feel a priori proofs were to be relegated to the dust bin of rationalist history. This view has been dramatically challenged in our own time by a host of thinkers, mainly as a result of the work of Charles Hartshorne. I am aware that an extensive literature on the proof, both pro and con, now exists. Since my concerns in this study are mainly with the empirical aspects of divinity, I have not attempted to deal with this literature. I have instead dealt with the main thrust of the proof as it appeared historically in St. Anselm and as it has been restated in our own time by Hartshorne. A great deal of the literature on this issue comes out of the analytic tradition and reflects considerable logical acumen and linguistic skill. Nevertheless, I still feel that unless one is touched by faith or intimation first, all attempts at a priori proofs reflect, at most, the logical ingenuity of the writer. I have a "gut level" feeling that existence of the divine must be arrived at from some aspect of experience or be derived from explicit commitment to revelation. My criticism of the ontological proof stems from a phenomenological empiricist orientation and not from the analytic tradition. Thus, I reject the pure a priori road, though, as we shall see, taking the ontological proof as a statement of faith rather than in the mode of proof, does provide profound insight into the God question. What we turn to then is a broad empirical approach to theism.

Within the empirical perspective there are a number of things which might be done. It would be possible to develop a metaphysics extrapolated from experience, with God as central in the manner of Whitehead or Weiss. This approach is very persuasive and it will be apparent to the reader how strongly indebted I am to Whitehead's basic position. I am also indebted to Charles Hartshorne, who has done some of the most significant writing on the God question in the last thirty years. While I have a major disagreement with Hartshorne over the ontological proof, the reader who is conversant with contemporary philosophy of religion will soon be aware that I owe a great deal of my own thinking to his inspiration. Hartshorne has tried more diligently and successfully than most to talk clearly and coherently about God. He has given profound insights to anyone interested in empirical theism though he himself is opposed to exclusive reliance on this position. While this study owes much to Hartshorne, I will take issue with him on the question of empirical theism and the ontological proof. Whitehead seems more congenial with empirical theism than does Hartshorne. Another thinker I feel very indebted to is William James. While not the most precise thinker who ever wrote, James has made major contributions to an empirically oriented philosophy of religion. I would like to think that this study is written "in the spirit of William James," with his sympathy and openness to the divine dimension combined with philosophical caution and deep religious concern.

While one possible approach is metaphysical, the other is what we might call phenomenological in character, and it is this latter aspect I would like to explore, combined with cautious epistemological explorations into the ontological domain. I will take certain "varieties of religious experience," describe them in phenomenological terms and then discuss them in terms of what I call <u>intimations</u> of divinity. I am making no claim to an exhaustive survey of religious experiences. On the contrary, only certain key aspects which lend themselves to a knowledge of the divine dimension will be studied. As aids in this preliminary phenomenological description I will draw on the phenomenological categories of Charles S. Peirce--Firstness, Secondness and Thirdness. We shall find as we proceed that they will prove helpful in our discussion of the aspects of human experience of the divine. While remaining close to Peirce's usage, I do not intend to follow it completely nor is my purpose to explicate the Peircean categories. I frankly intend to "borrow" them for my own purposes, but not, I hope, in a way which would do violence to Peirce's intent. From this background I wish to explore what cautious epistomological and metaphysical claims for religion might be made from what is broadly an empiricist base. My argument is that unless one truly makes an explicit appeal to revelation or commits oneself by an act of faith, experience gives us, at best, intimations of divinity. This is as far as empiricism can go, but these intimations are very significant. While it would require an act of faith to take you further, I will argue that religious faith is foolishness unless it is ultimately grounded in experience from which such intimations flow. It also seems highly likely that all deep religious faith is grounded in experience of divinity, whether it is explicitly recognized as such or not.

Something must be said about the problem of religious knowledge. A great deal has been done on this already, but the issue bears on our thesis about intimations of divinity. Anybody writing on epistemological questions today within the scope of even a broadened empiricism must recognize the impact that positivism and analytic philosophy have had in the last fifty years and, indeed, if one wants to push this inquiry further, the impact of the critical philosophy of the eighteenth century. While the high tide of positivism has receded, we are left with a new awareness that claims to knowledge legitimately require justification and that the most strongly supportable of knowledge claims reside in everyday life and in the formal and empirical sciences. One need not be a positivist to recognize this. One also need not be a devotee of logical empiricism or analytic philosophy to recognize that claims to knowledge about the existence and nature of God are problematic to say the least. Within the religious tradition it is recognized that God is a "hidden" God and outside the circle of faith God is so far from obvious that it is well within the bounds of reason to think there is no divine dimension to reality at all.

It is not until the widespread loss of faith in our own times that the oddity of theistic belief stands out clearly. Religious norms have dominated culture for so long that it has not been noticed that the divine dimension is far from obvious--at least not a great deal has been made of this. Putting the matter in its simplest terms, the existence of things and persons is obvious to all in a direct way in which God is not. What is involved here specifically will be spelled out in the chapters to come. Various claims to knowledge have differing degrees of epistemic force, depending on what the claim is. Unless one makes an explicit appeal to revelation it seems obvious that religious claims to knowledge lack the epistemic force of knowledge claims that occur in everyday life and science. In fact, I would argue that it is precisely the lack of epistemic coerciveness in the religious area that makes the appeal to faith appropriate. In everyday contexts we speak of having faith in something precisely where we lack knowledge. The language of belief and faith arises in any context where epistemic doubt is appropriate. I do not want to deny that there may be religious knowledge, but I do want to maintain that the epistemic force of religious knowledge claims is far down on the scale of many different kinds of knowledge claims, all with varying degrees of epistemic force.

It is worth keeping in mind that no claim to knowledge is absolutely coercive epistemically. This was the delusion entertained by many sense datum theorists and others who searched for the "holy grail" of the sheer "given" in experience. One is <u>always</u> at liberty to deny a knowledge claim, no matter how strong, by invoking auxiliary hypotheses or simply by the claim that one is dreaming or that what one is experiencing is an illusion. Also, with the collapse of the search for the given, it is seen that all knowledge involves some interpretive element on the human level--a point seen clearly by Peirce some time ago. Once this is recognized it is clear that while one could reject any claim to know, it would be highly unreasonable to do so in many contexts. While we can and do make religious claims to knowledge, it is never unreasonable to reject any such claim in the religious area. This is just an epistemological way of stating that religion is a matter of faith. Religious faith and belief are not irrational but they are clearly nonrational. I would argue that if we did not have intimations of divinity from experience, religious faith would lose much of its plausibility.

It is precisely because the epistemic force of claims to know God are so weak that I wish to introduce the idea of intimations of divinity. Empirically God is well hidden, and experience is frightfully ambiguous in the way it can be read. Yet it will be the main emphasis of this study that there are genuine intimations of divinity within experience from which it is legitimate to make cautious inferences about the existence and nature of God. If one wishes to make a stronger claim, which the religious believer can and must make, it must be done either on the basis of an explicit appeal to revealed truth and/or by an existential leap of faith. The intimations of divinity which can be found within experience, interpreting "experience" in the broadened sense in which James dealt with it, is a major concern of this study. My method of pursuit will be phenomenological, trying to depict the different aspects of experience which "point towards" a divine dimension. In the process of the discussion to come I shall also criticize the ontological proof. This is important for within the <u>philosophical</u> context one is either led towards God from experience or one must find a purely rational and a priori way to arrive at God. The defenders of the ontological proof are right in pointing out that a purely empirical theology lacks the epistemic force to give you the God of faith, but I think they are wrong in thinking that the a priori proof will do the job. As will be seen, I agree that a purely empirical theology <u>alone</u> is not adequate to accomplish the task of giving you the God of living faith, but without the groundwork of living experience involving intimations of divinity, faith is irrational, and without the groundwork of living experience the a priori road of the ontological proof becomes just an exercise in verbal sophistry. Given the groundwork of living experience, faith takes on a profound and important dimension and given the groundwork of living experience the ontological proof becomes a sublime statement of faith--a true "testament of devotion." In the course of discussing these issues I will also develop a distinction between two concepts--"divinity" and "God,"--the first being a purely phenomenological category and the second involving explicit ontological commitment. The direction in which we now must turn is the elucidation of these themes.

CHAPTER 1

SOME PERPLEXITIES CONCERNING GOD'S EXISTENCE

Much has been written about the nature of existence. Certain points concerning what it is to exist have not been brought out with sufficient clarity. The need for such clarity becomes apparent when the question of God's existence is raised. From the side of religion God would appear to function as a concrete entity and thus to exist in this manner. From the side of metaphysical speculation, God would appear to be known through concepts as a rational principle, abstract in nature. It will be my contention that while God is known as abstract in metaphysical contexts, he must be regarded primarily as a concrete entity, whose existence cannot be proved. The necessity for this view stems from certain difficulties which arise with the thought of those who support the ontological proof. In spite of acute criticism by Kant and others there are certain perplexities about what it means for things, persons and God to exist, perplexities with which I will deal in this chapter.

A principal part of what we mean when we speak of the existence of a thing or of a person is that there is a brute empirical "givenness" or presentation about it. One may attempt to capture what is given in one's conceptual network as it is given in experience, but the givenness is a presentation with which one must start. If people and things are "given," what happens when we say that God exists, particularly when God is used to rationalize the non-rational "given"? Of course there is also no "pure" given. We are always dealing with an interpretive given.

God has been conceived in many metaphysical systems as the ultimate rationale of what is, or exists. This point is brought out in the traditional cosmological argument: If God is the ultimate rationale for the surd aspects of contingent existence, then of course it makes no sense to ask for the rationale of God's existence, for he is the rationale itself. But I believe Kant's question can still be raised, namely that God might ask of himself, "But whence then am I?"[1] Those in the Anselmian and rationalist tradition would answer that to raise such a question is to fail to understand what it is to be God. They would say that God is the ultimate rationale of all that is and if his existence is necessary, then to raise a question of God's existence does not make sense, if one means by existence the brute contingency of givenness.

Modern empiricism finds it difficult to accept necessary existence in spite of the argument that God could not just happen to be, that is, <u>be</u> contingently, because the existence we are closest to is the existence of things and persons, and this kind of existence is simply given to us. But, it will be immediately retorted, God does not exist in this manner. Obviously God does not exist in the manner of either persons or things and because this is so, it is reasonable to conclude that God does not exist at all. Since God's existence is special, it is natural to try to justify it through some variant of the ontological argument, by revelation or by some inferential argument by analogy.

I want to suggest that God's existence must be <u>closer</u> to the givenness of persons and things than to the kind of existence which one attributes to theoretical constructs, inferred entities or some abstract necessary being arrived at by modal arguments from logic. Those who want to maintain the existence of God must start from some empirical base for their assertion. This is not to say that inference or analogical argument will be unnecessary, for that God is not <u>immediately</u> given is obvious enough; but the inference to God must lead to a <u>concrete</u> <u>entity</u> rather than to some kind of hypothetical construct or rational principle. One could seriously question whether God would have ever appeared as a metaphysical category or appeared in the ontological proof if certain major areas of human experience with which we are all familiar had not driven men, no matter how haltingly, towards this approach.

Extensive reading in mystical and religious literature conveys the impression that one is ontologically confronted by "something or other." This is not to say that these reports must be taken at face value or that one should not apply epistemological criticism, but it would be erroneous to assume that all such literature is poetic nonsense lacking any referential component. Once religious discourse is taken seriously, it would seem that divinity is assumed as given; it is simply taken for granted.

Religious language does not lend credence to the view that God's existence is analogous to hypothetical constructs or inferred scientific entities, nor to the view that God can be stipulated into existence by some variant of the ontological proof.

Though God's existence is not <u>immediately</u> given, still much religious language functions on the assumption that confrontation with the Divine occurs. This is admittedly vague, but it is difficult to know what more to say at this point. James speaks of this issue when he asserts that "the visible world is part of a more spiritual universe from which it draws its chief significance" and that "union or harmonious relation with that higher universe is our true end."[2] When religious language is taken as involving "report sentences," there seems to be, phenomenologically, a confrontation with an existent "something or other" of a spiritual nature. That this is an error is certainly possible, and we have only to read Hume's "Dialogues" to recall that any solid inference from the vague and numinous qualities of religious experience is risky. I am not trying to demonstrate God's existence, but if one already takes the existence of God seriously and approaches this matter in the context in which religious language rather than metaphysical language functions, then his existence must be <u>closer to</u> and more analogous to the simple givenness that we associate with the givenness of persons and things than to the type of "existence" which one might apply to a metaphysical principle. In short, the religious consciousness, not metaphysical thought, is our main source of data for theistic belief.

We may add to the above assertion that God comes to play various metaphysical roles in purely philosophical contexts as well. The metaphysical role that God plays is frequently at variance with the role that arises in the context of religious consciousness. The entity arrived at by the ontological proof in particular and the abstract principle of metaphysics in general is hardly a concrete being. "He" is a principle of sufficient reason, and, far from being given in the brute contingent sense, "he" is regarded in metaphysical contexts as the ultimate rationale of why there is anything contingent at all.

This is one of the main philosophical difficulties with the ontological proof. A necessary being or prime mover may be real or metaphysically <u>required</u> as a <u>principle</u> but it does not exist in the way we have been speaking of existence. Principles are used to explain what exists; they may be rationally required by a metaphysical system, but no givenness is involved here.

Thus, the statement "God exists" is logically odd. As an assertion of concrete existence it refers to something which is simply given, though obviously the givenness is interpreted, but the statement can also be taken in a metaphysical sense where the assertion is made that a metaphysical principle is required and that is all.

Aside from the fact that many persons are loath to

accept an a priori proof for God's existence, we ought to make very clear that any acceptance of a theistic argument must be supplemented by one or more of the following: truths of revelation, empirical suggestions from mystical and ordinary experience or further metaphysical speculation. Here Whitehead's procedure is preferable to that of Hartshorne, for Whitehead does not set out to prove God's existence. He develops metaphysical argumentation in combination with suggestive empirical considerations. Consequently, when God is arrived at, it is as a fully actual concrete being, exemplifying Whitehead's metaphysical categories. Hartshorne uses a variety of approaches too; my question is whether he puts too much emphasis on the ontological proof. Admittedly, our empirical knowledge of God is vague and tentative, more in the nature of intimations of divinity. Whatever information we can gain about God comes from such intimations. While it is true that clues to God's contingent aspects must be looked for in the spatio-temporal world, it does not follow that empirical knowledge gives us a full knowledge of God. While we can use empirical knowledge to make metaphysical extrapolations and tentative inferences of what God may be like, such a procedure is very tenuous and speculative at best.

To claim a "proof" for God's existence is far stronger than the contention that arguments for his existence can be given. It is obvious that many in the Anselmian tradition do not put all their eggs in one basket, for as Anselm said, "I believe in order to understand," not the other way around.

And yet, the term "proof" is too strong. Perhaps the revealed tradition in theology is much closer to the truth of the matter here than any of us suspect in its contention that God's grace is given, not proved. Thus, God's existence is a _gift_ also. I would generalize this notion and say that epistemologically the _existence_ of anything at all is a _gift_ in the sense that its presence is simply apprehended.

In the traditional view of Anselm, no distinction is made between essential and accidental properties in God. God may not be religiously adequate under traditional theism, as Hartshorne has shown so well, but he is certainly metaphysically complete as the ultimate and eternal ground of being. I find the Whitehead-Hartshorne view of dipolar theism much more religiously adequate than _traditional_ theism; but the introduction of any contingent aspect into the nature of God calls into serious question the goal of much traditional metaphysics, i.e., complete rationality and intelligibility. Dipolar theism maintains that God has both necessary and contingent aspects to his nature, whereas classical monopolar theism maintains that all properties are equally necessary in God--in short that God has no contingent aspects. Whitehead sees clearly that in some sense the being of God defies rational intelligibility when he speaks of God's existence as the ultimate irrationality.[3] God as a necessary being certainly can have contingent aspects, as Hartshorne argues. But a God with accidents is a different entity from that found in classical rationalist metaphysics. In the latter view a necessary being is completely self-contained, requiring nothing outside of itself. But this metaphysical being conflicts with the requirements of Christian theism, for the Christian God loves and love is a relation between entities. To love is to be partially dependent in some sense on the object of one's love.

Whitehead sees the limits to complete rational intelligibility. The goal of classical rationalism was a complete system, a system with no "loose ends." Whitehead is in the rationalist tradition, believing in the possibility of constructing an intelligible metaphysical system, but he realizes, as classical rationalism apparently did not, that any system must be open rather than closed and that further inquiry always requires revision. When Whitehead speaks of God's existence as the ultimate irrationality, he is not denying that God is basic to metaphysical explanation, but he is aware of the subtle point which escaped the rationalist tradition; the amazement over there being _anything at all_, God or world. Classical theism thought that a "sufficient reason" is required for there being a world, and assuming as it did that the world's existence was not self-explanatory, it grounded that existence in a necessary being. But classical theism never seemed to think it at all strange that there should be a God. Everything was completely rational once one had grounded the world in God. Kant and Whitehead seem to sense that both the world and God must be taken with "natural piety," whether as a postulate of practical reason or as in some sense "given" in the full richness of experience. This is not to say that they accept God as simply an irrational "surd" element, for they both believe in a rational approach to religion, but both appear to sense that there are limits to complete rationality. Yet once God is accepted as concrete and partially transparent to reason, there is no reason why he should not appear in metaphysical contexts. This is the breakthrough of dipolar theism. Classical theism seemed to involve itself in difficulties because it found it hard to unify the God of reason and the God of faith. The insight of dipolar theism is to see that God must be basically a concrete being, but this does not prevent the use of rational criteria applied to God, as far as they may be applicable.

In this problem of rationality, there is a sense in which the contingent as such is non-rationalizable. What is contingent or actual is what happens to be the case but is not necessary. Certainly the contingent is rationalizable if one means by this that it can be dealt with in terms of rational and/or scientific techniques. But the contingent is not fully rationalizable if one means by this that its reason for being is found within itself. The contingent is what we "find to be the case." It could have been otherwise. Now, admitted that there is a contingent aspect to God, namely his knowledge of what the facts of the world are, doesn't this mean that God cannot be completely rationalizable? This need not make God unintelligible, but it does mean that he is not completely transparent to reason. I have never known anyone who thought that God was simply a principle of reason and nothing else, and yet I have always found puzzling the assertion that one could think of God as satisfying the demand for <u>complete</u> rationality and intelligibility. God may help us better than anything else to satisfy this demand, but even God himself cannot ground contingency upon rationality in the manner of the cosmological argument, for a residue always remains. This is what Whitehead seems to be maintaining when he talks about God and ultimate irrationality.

From the religious side of the question, we have already argued that God's existence is more analogous to that of persons and things than to that of a principle, but if one wishes to try to develop a coherent philosophical view, one cannot ignore the rationalist demand for intelligibility incorporated in the search for a metaphysical first principle. While the Anselmian approach falls short of what it claims to produce, the driving metaphysical urge behind it must be dealt with.

By what methods might an abstract metaphysical principle be identified with an existent God? This is an extremely difficult problem and we can only make some tentative suggestions here. One might approach the matter by taking the "ontological proof" <u>in conjunction with</u> the belief in a concrete actuality arrived at in a different way, and then try to draw the two parts together. Hartshorne can be interpreted as trying to do this when he contends that God as a necessary existent must always have some actual state or other, but that the particular concrete state of God's knowledge at any particular time is a contingent matter. But Hartshorne's position is more ambitious than this, because he claims we have a valid proof of the existence of <u>God</u>. In Hartshorne's view, one must distinguish between God's essential and God's accidental properties--as he would put it, between God's existence and his actuality.[4] This closely parallels Whitehead's distinction between God's primordial nature and consequent nature. Hartshorne maintains that God's existence is necessary but that God in his full <u>actuality</u> possesses contingent aspects as well. For Hartshorne and Whitehead this constitutes God in his full and actual concrete nature.

There is a difficulty in speaking of God's necessary existence <u>as distinct</u> from his full actuality when one seeks, as Hartshorne does, to support a variant of the ontological proof. It would be better, perhaps, to speak of the ontological <u>aspect</u> of divinity rather than of a proof, for with a "proof" or "argument" it is generally assumed that the full "object" of theistic inquiry, namely God, follows. At best, the ontological argument simply produces an abstraction. What the Anselmian "proof" does is seemingly establish a necessarily existent being, but such a being falls short of an actual God. God as a concrete being must be actual, and his actuality can only be given when one takes into consideration his contingent attributes, and these cannot be given by the ontological proof.

Hartshorne, no doubt, would reply that it is a sufficient

accomplishment to establish that there _is_ a necessary being, fully actual. After all, in many inquiries it is sufficient to establish that there exists such and such an entity satisfying such and such a function, without going on to specify the entity in detail. I am also aware that Hartshorne wants to maintain that it is necessary that God exists as fully actual and concrete. God must always have some concrete actual state, but the _particular_ actual state of God at any time is contingent and not necessary. For example, it is necessary that God knows fully whatever actually is the case, but it is a contingent fact of God's knowledge that he knows that Elizabeth Taylor married Richard Burton.

But Hartshorne has not by-passed the really significant criticisms which can be made of any form of the ontological proof, namely that one cannot go from concepts to real existence. Hartshorne claims that Kant and other critics have completely missed the point which Anselm was trying to make, the point that _God could not simply happen to be_, that is, exist contingently. But if one takes this tack, he assumes what he sets out to prove. If one starts out by saying that God _logically could not_ exist contingently, then as Hartshorne points out, _modally_, God's existence is logically impossible or his existence is necessary. Since there seems no self-contradiction in the concept of God, his necessary existence follows at once. But one is left with the uneasy feeling that in all forms of the ontological proof there is a conceptual tour-de-force. I hasten to add that once one sets aside this matter of proving God's existence, what Hartshorne has to say about God is very significant. His distinction between God's existence and his actuality is a strikingly profound insight about our knowledge of God as a fully concrete being. The distinction, similar to Whitehead's, between God's primordial and consequent nature is valuable conceptually. Perhaps what Hartshorne is maintaining is that the ontological proof can tell us that it is necessary that there exists an x such that x satisfies the function, divine being; the proof itself, being abstract, points to a being which is fully concrete. My criticism is that the proof cannot work at all unless one is <u>already</u> confronted by the concrete being, in which case a proof is superfluous. I think I understand what Hartshorne wants to say, but I use the distinction between existence and actuality to deny his point. Both of us want to use the term "existence" to designate a fully actual being, but the distinction between existence and actuality brings out more sharply, I think, where the proof breaks down. Hartshorne wants to maintain that the proof is of God's necessary existence as a fully actual being. My purpose in stressing this distinction between existence and actuality is to use it in a different way--that is, to point up the view that at best a proof can only give us an abstraction.

There seems to be a lack of sufficient sensitiveness to the notion that the concrete empirical <u>existence</u> or actuality of anything, be it man, stone or God, must in some sense be derived from experience. Once one "has God," so to speak, one may then through reason come to the conclusion that God may fit the dipolar description which Whitehead gives of him. Hartshorne might reply that once one sees what it means to be God, it will be apparent that God exists necessarily. There are several possible rejoinders to this. One is to follow Whitehead's dipolar theism rather than Hartshorne's. We can accept the distinction between God's primordial nature and consequent nature without including necessary existence as a part of his nature. It might be helpful to refer to C. S. Peirce's category of "Secondness,"[5] which involves a dyadic relation. Secondness occurs when one thing "comes up against" another thing. In terms of human existence, while related to the world and to other persons, we remain distinct from them. We confront another, and another confronts us. Whether this other be a thing or a human being, Secondness is involved. In this way one might say that we come upon God; God confronts us, not immediately to be sure, but in some sense. It is this profound insight that the notion of a priori theistic proof seems to obscure. It is for this reason that I feel unable to accept any variant of the ontological proof, including Hartshorne's. One must seriously question whether anything "we come up against" or confront must exist by logical necessity.

Whitehead does not consider it important to "prove" that God exists. He does indicate that the only possible proof for the existence of God would seem to be the ontological proof,[6] but he goes on to point out that most philosophers and theologians reject this proof, and he seems to let the matter rest at that. His approach is more fruitful than others we have been discussing for the following reasons: it is true that God appears in a metaphysical context and performs essential metaphysical functions in the system, but there is room for stress on the givenness of God which we found absent in the Anselmian approach. For one thing, God is an actual entity, which indicates that he is one of the concrete entities of Whitehead's system. There are difficulties in treating God as an actual entity, the main difficulty being that God endures whereas other actual entities do not. The reason for mentioning the point here is that in calling God an actual entity, Whitehead seems to intend that we regard him as a fully concrete being and not as an abstract principle. Also, Whitehead's theistic views and arguments come out of and reflect his own religious experience and that of others, the only source where God's givenness can be found.

Another perplexity about the position maintained by Anselmians is that any God that fails to exist necessarily would fail of being God, would fail to be an adequate object of religious worship. Their contention is that either God is a necessary being or the idea of God does not make sense and is self-contradictory on both metaphysical and religious grounds. Metaphysical requirements aside for the moment, why could not a very powerful and good but nevertheless contingent God be an adequate object for religious worship? Part of the difficulty is that the requirements of religious adequacy are psychological in that what one man finds adequate another does not. It would seem that a minimum requirement for an adequate object of devotion is the belief in a beneficent force or forces in the universe, independent of man, to which one may address prayers and supplications with some hope and expectation of satisfaction.

One might counter that there are degrees of adequacy and that the difference between a higher and a lower religion is that the former sees clearly that a fully adequate object of religious devotion must be a necessary being. Even if one granted this, I do not see <u>in terms of the criteria of religious adequacy alone</u> that the idea of a contingent God is self-contradictory or nonsensical. James and others have embraced such doctrines. Of course we have no clear knowledge about God's ontological status. It seems to be the case that God could either be or not be. Atheism may indeed be false, but it seems highly implausible to agree with the Anselmians that atheism is a self-contradictory doctrine. "Only the fool can say in his heart there is no God" while applicable to dogmatic atheism, is much too cavalier a judgement to make of serious and concerned agnosticism. In terms of the study of religious phenomena, it would seem that the distinction between a necessary and a contingent God is not of primary importance or of much concern. What those in the Anselmian tradition might maintain is that philosophically considered, a necessary being is the only kind that can be a fully adequate object of religious devotion, particularly if one adds metaphysical requirements for intelligibility and rationality. Are issues concerning God and the universe this clear and distinct? Perhaps Whitehead's remark that God is the ultimate irrationality reflects a sound religious instinct for the mysterious in the Divine. One need not adopt the view that no rational approaches can be made to the Divine, that it is all purely a matter of irrational faith, but in some sense the open approach on this matter that one finds in Whitehead appears closer to the religious consciousness than the clear necessity set forth by those in the Anselmian tradition.

Much analytic work has been done on the ontological proof over the last thirty years; as I have indicated I do not intend to get into this because I am concerned with developing an empirical and phenomenological approach and the a priori road remains purely on the a priori level. No matter how well worked out such approaches are, they fall victim to the empirical insight that when it comes to things, persons and God, one cannot establish existence by remaining at the conceptual level.

NOTES

1 Immanuel Kant, Critique of Pure Reason, trans. Norman Kemp Smith (New York: The Macmillan Company, 1929) p. 513. Father Norris Clarke in correspondence with me points out that the theistic tradition would not regard it as a meaningful question for God to ask of himself "Whence then came I?" or for anybody else to ask it concerning God. The theistic tradition is committed to the view that the universe is ultimately intelligible in that God is the sufficient reason for the universe and its intelligibility. Anything less than God has some deficiencies that force us to continue our inquiry. The postulation of, or faith in God would presumably bring inquiry to an end, for God would have no deficiencies and would be the source of ultimate intelligibility. I have a basic philosophical disagreement with the theistic tradition on this point. It has always been hard for me to understand the use of "intelligibility" by those who invoke a principle of sufficient reason. If it means that everything becomes clear or that it makes no sense to pursue inquiry further once one has arrived at God, then I find it difficult to accept. What seems glaringly apparent is that the further we pursue both scientific and philosophical inquiry, the more unintelligible things become or to put it more positively--as we know more, the area of the mysterious and the surd extends. It is a main contention of this study that God is indeed the *most* mysterious and peculiar entity of all and far from being

a source of ultimate intelligibility, God, as Whitehead says, is the ultimate irrationality. Father Clarke is right that first cause and sufficient reason are often confused; see his "A Curious Blindspot in the Anglo-American Tradition of Anti-Theistic Argument" in The Monist, Vol. 54, April 1970. In short, the theistic tradition has a rationalistic faith in the ultimate intelligibility of the universe which I do not share, due to the brute character of givenness, the mystery of it all and various intimations of cosmic absurdity, which run counter to the intimations of divinity I am concerned with.

[2] William James, Essays in Pragmatism (New York: Hafner Publishing Co., 1948) p. 110.

[3] A. N. Whitehead, Science and the Modern World (New York: Mentor Books, 1963) p. 160.

[4] Charles Hartshorne and William Reese, Philosophers Speak of God (Chicago: University of Chicago Press, 1953) pp. 104-105.

[5] Charles Hartshorne and Paul Weiss, eds., Collected Papers of Charles Sanders Peirce, (Cambridge, MA: Harvard University Press, 1960) 1. 23-26, 325.

[6] A. N. Whitehead, Religion in the Making (New York: Meridian, 1960) p. 68.

CHAPTER 2

WHAT THE ONTOLOGICAL PROOF CAN AND CANNOT DO

There are things the ontological proof cannot do. While God's status is unique because his nature is different from ordinary contingent things, even God cannot be brought conceptually into being by the pure rational insight of the proof. If the ontological argument gives an accurate reading of what the sincere believer comes to accept, then isn't the proof sound since part of what it maintains is that full insight into the nature of God makes us see that he must exist? Insight on the part of the believer that God is unique does not mean that God has been proved. There are two modes of assertion in which the Anselmian insight is uttered. One is in the mode of a mathematical demonstration, the other is in the mode of an address of faith to God. The first is illegitimate and sophistical, the second is legitimate and profound.

As a proof it cannot work, for a proof from concepts is addressed to all rational beings whether they have faith or not. If it does work, what is proved is proved once and for all to rational beings who go through the steps of the proof. A proof, to be acceptable of course, does not have to be acceptable to all men. Many have rejected logically sound arguments through ignorance, dogmatism or carelessness. Thus, that many reject the Anselmian argument psychologically is beside the point. The difficulty is more profound than this.

If the argument genuinely worked as a proof, the issue would be settled once and for all. Yet Kant and many other thinkers balked at the notion that the proof is logically coercive. One does not expect all people to be moved by a rational demonstration, but I have never heard of <u>anyone</u> who was converted to theism from non-theism on the basis of the rational argument of the proof alone. I can imagine Anselm's argument pushing someone over the edge, who had already "come clear" in his mind that there is a God, on other grounds--but it is the other grounds, be they revelation or experience which produces the conviction, not the proof. Kant's profound point is a logical one and is the main one, which indicates failure of the argument as demonstration. One cannot go from concepts to real existence, even on the divine level. A man deeply committed to God through faith, readily will assent to the idea that God's modal status is unique--that obviously God could not just happen to be another item of furniture in the world. On the other hand if one looks at the bare bones of a rational argument (outside the context of faith), just being told that God as necessary must exist will only produce the impression of patent sophistry. This may seem like splitting hairs but I think there is a profound point to be made here. The tendency has been either to accept the ontological argument as sound and valid or to look on it with incredulity that intelligent men should engage in such nonsense. Neither attitude is the correct one. The validity of an argument or proof should have nothing to do with whether one is inside or outside of a faith context.

If, as Anselm says, you must believe in order to understand, then you don't have a proof and you just confuse things by trying to pretend that you do. On the other hand, the continuing appeal of the ontological argument indicates that something more than nonsense is involved here. What is involved is seen most clearly in Anselm's formulation where it appears in the context of an address to God as an act of faith. As a profound statement of what the believer feels in his heart, the lasting impact of the ontological argument is a "testament of devotion." The history and downfall of the argument is from a "testament of devotion" to a logical exercise, though in fairness I must say that, though I disagree with him, to Hartshorne himself, it is a "testament of devotion" as well as a logical argument.

I have indicated briefly what the ontological argument cannot do. Let me spend more time indicating what it can do. Aside from being a profound statement of faith it can serve to help "fill out" the content of an empirically based theology. While empirical theology is a necessary foundation for theism, it needs supplementation by other means. A strict empiricism alone cannot give you a coherent interpretation of anything, as Hume's brilliant attempt showed. Thought must and does enter the empirical process. Experience of the divine is the impetus for theism and the great wealth of literature of religious experience is testimony to this impetus, but the wealth of the literature also abounds with vagueness and inconsistency. In the attempts to interpret these experiences intelligibly, concepts of the divine have undergone refinement from the days of primitive animism to the present. Over the centuries many sensitive religious people came to feel that the categories of the divine and the holy represented something special and unique. The feeling grew that although the object of worship manifested itself in experience, nevertheless God was not an ordinary piece of the furniture of the universe--that in some peculiar sense he was uniquely supreme. The feeling grew that an ordinary contingent being is not an adequate object of worship religiously or metaphysically. Religiously there were many reasons for thinking of God as preeminently unique. The felt qualities of the <u>mysterium tremendum</u> that Otto talks about--the sense of dread and awe where one cannot see God and live, were prime factors. The religious demand that God be all loving and dependable in an absolute sense, was a requirement that no ordinary contingent being, no matter how good, could fulfill. The very idea of a supreme being itself pointed towards a unique status, because again, for any ordinary contingent being C, no matter how powerful and good, it would logically be possible that at some time or other there would be another contingent being C^1 which would surpass C.

The main danger seemed to be that the demands put on the concept of divinity seemed to drive such a being out of the empirical and contingent realm altogether. In short, the utter transcendence of God threatened to reduce him to a pure construct of reason. This is the pitfall into which religious rationalism and exclusive emphasis on doctrinal revelation fall. When the lead strings to experience are cut, then religion becomes simply a matter of propositional assent to statements about a supposed supreme being who is forever remote. Yet if one remains at the level of pure immanence and empirical mysticism one can scarcely get further than vague feelings of superior powers--intimations of divinity if you will, which while essential to the life blood of religion, are not sufficient for a fully matured religious consciousness. Thus, quite rightly, a number of religious thinkers have maintained that immanence and transcendence must both be maintained in God--that while God must be grounded in the empirical, there is a uniqueness and tremendousness about the divine which reason must try to explicate.

At its profoundest level, the ontological argument is a rational attempt to explicate and interpret the awe-inspiring impact with the divine dimension in experience. It attempts to give some interpretive content to the profound feelings for the divine which occur at the deeper levels of religious experience. As in the case of Anselm and others, the argument is a product of those on whom the impact of God is considerably stronger than one of gentle intimation. It represents the thinking of those who have felt the full impact of God or else it represents those who, taking the conventional attributes of divinity to heart, have regarded necessary existence as a logical consequence. It is experience such as Otto talks about, where God is experienced as the *mysterium tremendum*, that leads one towards the explication involved in the Anselmian argument. Let's put it this way: by the "logic of faith," to one touched by God, it becomes obvious that "that than which nothing greater can be conceived" must exist necessarily. And to such a person an adequate conceptualization would seem to be that involved in the ontological argument.

It might be retorted at this point that what I have come up with is something like the doctrine of twofold truth, and that this is just as sophistical an "out" as that was. Outside the circle of faith, the ontological argument is sophistry and within the circle of faith it is religiously sound, if not logically coercive. But is not truth of a single cloth? What makes us recoil from the twofold doctrine of truth is precisely that truth is one; you cannot have it both ways. There either is a necessary being or there isn't. If the so-called ontological argument is invalid as proof, then the devout person who thinks that God exists necessarily is deluded, no matter how pious he feels. We must avoid being clear-cut in an area where at best we "see through a glass darkly." One of the main drawbacks of the ontological argument as proof is that it attempts to be clear-cut in an area where much is unavoidably hidden. One should seek for as much precision as one can get in this area, but in matters of faith one can only go so far without becoming dogmatic. The blunt fact is that nobody knows (in any reasonable coercive sense) whether there is a God at all, or if there is, what his precise nature may be. The whole thrust of my case is that we have intimations of divinity which are persistent and widespread enough to be taken seriously. If it were not for the intimations of divinity reported by mystics, poets and ordinary people through the years, speculation on the divine would be idle speculation, but far from being idle, such speculation is of vast importance and it is important that it be done carefully and well. Such speculation done carefully will help fill out the intimations of divinity we have with "flesh and bones."

What must be rejected is a twofold doctrine of truth. I am not arguing that the ontological argument is <u>valid</u> religiously and <u>invalid</u> philosophically. I am arguing that the ontological argument is invalid, <u>period</u>, but that it is not therefore nonsense or pure sophistry when taken in the context of faith. I am concerned with what the argument can and cannot do, not with whether it is valid. I have argued that it cannot "do" what many of its proponents have claimed for it--namely provide a proof of God. But it can "do" a great deal more, which many who argue about it pro and con are but dimly aware of. It not only can provide an additional assurance to the man of faith, it can provide insight to the religious philosopher who is willing to use philosophical speculation as a tool in developing a reasonable and coherent doctrine of God. Since empirical theology by itself is inadequate,[1] God cannot be just another ordinary item of furniture in the world. What then, may God be like?

This is where the Anselmian approach may be of help. A main function of the Anselmian approach is to show that God is a unique being. Most theologians and philosophers of religion seem agreed that God is not simply another being among beings. Orthodoxy seems to be correct on the point that God is unsurpassable by anything else. This is where a purely empirical theology such as James' needs supplementation by rational conceptual argumentation. The important point here is supplementation. A reading of any of the major thinkers will show that this is so. Our religious feelings and experiences make us feel that God is "something special." It is our rational speculation that indicates more specifically what this "something special is." The ontological argument maintains that this special quality is necessary existence. Put in this bald a form we have the proof and we have already rejected it as proof.

Let us see if we could not accept Anselm's thrust in a somewhat different sense. As a "testament of devotion" on the part of the believer, what is asserted is that the absence of God is inconceivable. God may be absent from the believer in the sense that he is hidden, but he still exists, ready at the time and place of his own choosing to manifest himself to the believer again. "God is that than which nothing greater can be conceived" gives testimony to the utter reliance of the believer on the divine. No such statement could be made of any item of furniture in the world or any collection of such items, including the world itself. This is what the so-called ontological argument can do. It can and does give rational expression to the deep faith of the believer. One only has to read Anselm himself to be deeply moved by this expression of faith, and the logic of what he is doing is somehow clear to Anselm when he says that he believes in order to understand. The order is important here; it is not the other way around. One only has to reverse the order and compare the Cartesian formulation with that of Anselm to see the difference. Descartes must understand in order to believe, and his formulation is a caricature compared to that of Anselm--the same kind of caricature performed by contemporary logicians who try to make the proof "work." Now we must examine further and see why God must be given unique status.

The unique status of God centers around what it is to be an adequate object of worship, and what a full realization of religious adequacy involves. In the history of religions it will be found that all kinds of things have been worshipped at one time or another. One need not recapitulate that history here. In the course of time all these various objects and persons came to be considered as inadequate objects of worship. Why? One main factor is that the worshipper came to surpass the object of worship in some crucial respect. The sun while it is the source and sustainer of life became inadequate ultimately because it could not respond as a person to persons. It possesses no aesthetic or moral sensitivity and, thus, could not meet the needs of persons in this area.

For the same kind of reason persons found physical objects in the world and the world itself inadequate objects of worship, because people surpassed them in crucial ways, in aesthetic, ethical and religious sensitivity, and such objects could not minister to such needs. Pascal saw this point quite clearly when he maintained that though the world could crush man like a reed, man was superior to the world in that he was a thinking reed. Thus, any object incapable of thought is already inadequate to fulfill the needs of the worshipper, and while it may take thousands of years for the worshipper to find this out, sooner or later human sophistication will brand such objects as inadequate and the worship of such as idolatry. Such objects may be loved, admired and coveted, but worship is something else. The same situation holds for the worship of other persons. Any person, no matter who he may be, because of his finite nature is surpassable by another. One may love and cherish other persons, but no person can live up to the burden of worship--sooner or later they will fail in some crucial area. Human moral and religious sensitivity will demand more than the other person can possibly give, and the same argument holds for the attempt to worship any state or society.

It is beside the point to argue that people worship all kinds of things at the moment and feel that they are adequately fulfilled in doing so. The point is that any item of furniture in the world, including the world itself, is fallible, and will be subject to failure as human sensitivity and growth develop and require more. The history of religions is littered with the wrecks of gods which have failed; indeed, secular history itself is replete with examples of such failures. It is this kind of insight that is behind the thrust of Tillich's contention that God cannot be a being among beings. It is this insight that Anselm had when he maintained that God must be the greatest conceivable being--that he must be unsurpassable, or as Hartshorne maintains, surpassable only by himself. To us, God has a unique status because once we have thought this matter through, we see that the only adequate object of worship is one that is in principle unsurpassable by the worshipper, no matter how subtly developed his aesthetic, moral and religious sensitivity becomes. Sensitive persons in all religious traditions have found that God is not a tribal god, that he does not favor some persons over others as a group, that he is not warlike. Any finite object falls before the increasing sensitivity of mankind. Only the in-principle unsurpassable will do. This is the insight that the ontological argument provides and this is why the doctrine of a contingent empirical god, not filled out with rational criteria of adequacy, will fail.

Aren't we saying again in a roundabout way that God's special property is necessary existence, and, thus, supporting the argument as proof? For myself I would say no, for God's existence is just as much a mystery as the existence of anything else. At this crucial point I part company with the

Anselmians. Existence, secular or divine, is an ultimate surd and must be derived from experience. God's existence is not self-explanatory any more than the existence of anything else. Existence of anything including God must be accepted with "animal faith." Classical rationalism sought to ignore this point by regarding God's existence as necessary and self-authenticating. It is not God's existence per se which is unique but his nature once he is presented to the religious consciousness.

I would rather follow Whitehead at this point. God's unique mode is not necessary existence, rather it is that he alone has a primordial nature as well as a consequent nature. In his primordial nature, God's outreach and love is infinite and is not dependable more-or-less, but dependable absolutely. No matter what the demands of human nature may be in the future, God in his infinite capacity can fulfill them. This is the truth behind Anselm's approach.

One must add here, however, that all I have said is meaningless and idle speculation unless one has been touched by the divine in human experience first. Once the divine has manifested itself in human experience to the degree that humans recognize it as such, then such speculations as these may help to add some content to experience. All experience is interpretive as Peirce well knew. What we have been developing is the interpretive component--but the experience and the interpretation must go together. Either one without the other is empty. This interpretation may be grossly inadequate. Let the reader try another that arises out of his own experience. And if there is no experience that is interpretable in religious categories? Then what we have done is nothing more than idle chatter, but one must be bold indeed to deny the possibilities of such experience.

NOTES

[1] See Chapter 3.

CHAPTER 3

THE INADEQUACY OF A PURELY EMPIRICAL THEOLOGY

Let us now look at <u>empirical</u> theism in terms of its philosophical and religious adequacy. A major criticism which has been directed at any kind of empirical theism comes from Hartshorne.[1] He maintains that any kind of strictly empirical theism would make God a contingent being, different in degree perhaps from other contingent beings, but not different in kind. Any purely contingent being, by its very nature would not be God and the worship of such a being would be idolatry. Thus, if Hartshorne is right one could never arrive at God from the premises of a strict empirical theism.

One could point to Hume's famous "Dialogues" at this point as indicating just how far short of God you fall by trying to use empirical premises. This is seen in his famous criticism of the Design argument. Under this argument the most you could get would be a kind of divine architect of the universe, a senile deity, or a deity learning how to create worlds. Hume's criticisms would seem to indicate clearly that to arrive at a doctrine of God, remotely approaching that of the Judeo-Christian tradition, one would have to go to that tradition explicitly or use some argument such as Anselm's. Combine this with Hartshorne's contention that a contingent being could not be God and one has a strong refutation of attempts to build an <u>exclusively</u> empirical doctrine of theism.

From the perspective of this criticism let us examine

empirical approaches trying to see first why they would have been developed and secondly trying to reevaluate their religious and philosophical adequacy. The attempt to develop an empirical philosophy of religion should have even more appeal in our time than in times past. Revealed religion seems irrelevant, doctrinaire and arbitrary to increasing numbers of people. This of course does not prove that it is so, but it is a fact that the road of revelation seems an increasingly hard one for educated people to take. One difficulty here is what you do with conflicting revelations.

Mysticism's contribution to religion is its insistence on an experiential foundation for theism. It is this insight that William James tries to formulate and develop in his writings about God and religious experience. At this point we must say something about the term "experience." If one is going to apply the term in religious contexts it is obviously broader than its usage within what has generally been called the empiricist tradition. There are precise senses of "experience" which have been defined in Kantian, positivistic or other terms. We choose to use the term in the same spirit and sense in which James used it. We are obviously not subsuming sense contents under concepts in this discussion. In dealing with the empirical approach to theism, we wish to look at religious experience, at least to start, in the careful phenomenological sense in which James took it when he drew his cautious conclusions to <u>The Varieties of Religious Experience</u>.[2] At this level it is clear that one does not have anything approaching a full-fledged Christian theism. One has, as James puts it, a sense of the continuity of our consciousness with a larger consciousness of which it is a part. Even at the conclusion of the Varieties James is careful to keep the discussion on what we would call the phenomenological level, avoiding explicit ontological commitment.

Let us broaden the scope of this discussion and pass from phenomenological description to ontological commitment, as the mystics would do immediately. Let us assume at this point, for the purposes of discussion, that since we feel at certain moments that our consciousness is continuous with a larger consciousness, it is a fact that there is a larger consciousness with which our consciousness is continuous. Such a larger consciousness would, empirically, be a contingent being as much as other contingent beings. Let us call this larger consciousness C. No matter with what impact we encounter C, no matter how much our experience of C may be qualified by laudatory value predicates, we have at best encountered another item of furniture in the world. Unusual, exciting and all important to us in a value sense, C will still be another contingent being along with other contingent beings. Of all the things in the world, C may rank at the top of the scale of values in the sense of being more valuable than anything else we experience, but C will nevertheless remain contingent.

Given this state of affairs, is there any reason to

equate C with God, as the divine being has been more or less traditionally conceived? The obvious answer would seem to be "no." God must have special modal status to be God and to equate C with God would be to engage in the grossest of category mistakes. This has been the judgment of most of the tradition from Anselm through Thomas to Tillich and Hartshorne. On the empirical level alone, the properties of C are much too vague to be equated with God. James, in a very cautious way, seems to draw the minimal conclusion from the evidence provided by his varieties of religious experience. The most that James is willing to say, on the basis of the evidence afforded, is that we are in contact with something which we have characterized as C--a larger consciousness continuous with our own. At a later stage, James is willing to identify C with a more determined concept of God. James and others, on the basis of religious experience and inference from that experience, have developed doctrines of empirical theism. No matter which concept of God you deal with, whether it be that of James, Brightman, Wieman or somebody else, since the concept is empirically derived, the referent of the concept would seem to be a contingent being, and the criticism is that a contingent being cannot be an adequate object of worship and cannot be identified with God. Why not?

The answer generally given is that a contingent being (C) depends on something outside of itself in order to exist. It does not exist always; it comes into being and goes out of being--that is to say it exists at some time or other, but not at all times. Furthermore for any C there is no ultimate reason why C should ever exist at all. Its existence, if it occurs at all, just happens to be the case, and its existence is completely dependent on factors outside of itself. Depending on what C is, it may be loved, admired, hated, coveted, sought after, but it is not an adequate object of worship; if C is worshipped, this act would be one of idolatry pure and simple. Thus, C is never to be identified with God, though sinful people through all time have attempted to identify some C or other with God. An adequate object of worship cannot be one which just happens to come into being, and at some time or other, depending on circumstances, may cease to be. This is seen in the religious demand that God be absolutely dependable, no matter what. This is a requirement which no ordinary contingent being could fulfill. Furthermore, for any contingent being, even if it be a super-person and loves others now, it is at least logically possible that it might grow tired of others over time, that others might drive it insane or that it might die. All this makes sense when applied to contingent beings, but the tradition will maintain that it makes no sense to think such things of God. Orthodoxy would maintain that in the tradition of empirical theism it would make sense to say "God is dead," but that an adequate theology would understand that the phrase is self-contradictory since God is a necessary being.

The most cogent criticism which might be made of the doctrine of a contingent God would be the following. Of any two contingent beings x and y it is logically possible that at some time or other x could surpass y in ability to love, respond, manifest power and, likewise, that y could surpass x in the same way. A consequence of this kind of empirical theism is that it would be logically possible that the contingent world in whole or in part might at some time or other surpass God in power, love and the ability to respond. Charles Hartshorne has made the point very clearly that it is essential that God be surpassable <u>only by himself</u> at a future state. Thus, again, God would seem to be a necessary, not a contingent being. Earlier concepts of God were idolatrous and became clearly inadequate as concepts of divinity. Any morally sensitive human being such as Socrates was seen to be superior to Zeus and the whole tribe of Gods on Mt. Olympus. Earlier concepts of divinity were given up because human spiritual and moral sensitivity soon surpassed such concepts--humans were morally superior to gods. Even if one develops a concept of God on an empirical base which surpasses what humans can now achieve or think of achieving, if such a being is conceived contingently, it remains logically possible that at some time or other human spiritual sensitivity might surpass such a being. Thus, such a conceived being could not be God. Thus, again, God would have to be conceived non-empirically as that being which is unsurpassable by anything except himself in some future state. God must be intrinsically superior to all contingent beings--he must be superior in principle, not just in fact; therefore, any attempt to develop a purely empirical theism is bound to be misconceived.

This is a very strong and cogent criticism. It would seem that the question raised as to whether an empirical theology is adequate or not should be answered in the negative. Metaphysically, empirical theism would seem to be inadequate because God must be given a unique category unto himself. A contingent God would also be religiously inadequate for it would seem implausible to worship a being that might cease to exist, that might lose interest or which one might conceivably surpass. Yet when all is said and done what can be said for empirical theology? To turn one's back on the tradition of empirical theism is a mistake--we have much to learn from it even though we may have to reject it as the last word in theism.

The question of what an adequate object of religious worship is _psychologically_ is not an easy or precise notion to explicate. What may be adequate for one person may not be adequate for another. What does seem apparent here is that a contingent being (C) could very well appear to be an adequate object of worship _psychologically_ for many people. Only theologians and philosophers talk about adequacy, contingency and necessity. Most worshippers worship the object of their devotion without thinking about this question at all. But all this says is that idolatry is actual and is practiced by people who do not even know it is idolatry and who couldn't care less. Thus, the question of what is psychologically an adequate object of worship is not very helpful in discussing empirical theism. Many people feel drugs are adequate, but this says nothing as to whether they really are or not. The significant issue is that orthodoxy will maintain that no contingent being is _metaphysically_ an adequate object of worship, regardless of what the worshipper may think, for the reasons we mentioned earlier. To base the question of religious adequacy on necessary _existence_, however, is a mistake. While God is not a necessary existent, he is not an ordinary run-of-the-mill contingent being either. God's ontological status is unique, but does contain contingent aspects.

It is precisely at this point that the importance of empirical approaches to theism becomes relevant. At this point I revert strongly to the spirit of James' broadened empiricism. For both the believer and the unbeliever, _experience_ is a crucial factor in discussing God or anything else worthwhile. While God may be uniquely categorized, this does not mean that he is purely and only a creature of revealed doctrine or of rational argument. It is the _exclusively_ latter approach which makes so much talk about God seem sterile and academic. James and the mystics are right--unless the concept of God is derived in some sense from experience, the whole exercise is pointless. Thus, while empirical theology is clearly inadequate in certain important respects, we will not have given it its fair due by simply answering our opening question negatively. It is inadequate if it stands alone, but empiricism is essential to any healthy and coherent theistic viewpoint. It is the positive aspect of the task to which we must now turn.

The lifeblood of religion is direct encounter with the divine. While theology may explicate the nature of God, it would remain a purely formal and empty discipline unless it were constantly renewed by firsthand religious experience. While most religious believers are not mystics, the phenomenon of religious experience is much more widespread than might be supposed both inside and outside the confines of religious orthodoxy. The attempt to explicate this experience in rational terms has produced the classical arguments for God's existence and the discussion about the modality of that existence. Remove this experiential source and these discussions stand out as sterile and empty. This is why the man untouched by faith quite rightly rejects the arguments as attempts to convince him. You can discuss these questions rationally and philosophically, but they do not make any sense unless one has been touched by faith and then what such discussion does is explicate what the believer has already felt through direct experience. One must be careful here. <u>The experience does not prove God</u> any more than the rational argument does. The rational explication carries conviction to the man touched by faith as indicating what he deeply feels already.

William James is one of our most underrated and unduly neglected thinkers. There are many incisive insights throughout his writings and nowhere is he better than in his insistence on the importance of experience as a basis for religion. His classic work on the varieties of religious experience plus his own spiritual searching bears this out. If one simply says that empirical theology is inadequate and leaves it at that, one does this type of theology a great injustice. To paraphrase from another context one might say that if theology does not end in experience, it must begin with experience. This is the great lesson of James. His significance lies not only in his deep appreciation for the religious dimension of experience, but his willingness to try to draw some conclusions from the wealth of data which he collected on religious experiences.

In dealing with the varieties of experience which occur in different traditions, he finds a common nucleus running through the testimony to the effect that the mystics feel there is something wrong with us in our natural condition and that a solution whereby we may be saved from this condition does exist.[3] There is also general agreement that there is something "more" than simply our finite consciousness--that there is a larger consciousness of some kind which really exists, though there is of course disagreement as to the nature of this larger consciousness. At one level James is aware that this "more" may be viewed as a continuation of our conscious selves on the unconscious level. He knows that there is more to our total self than we are at any time aware of. At the same time James does not share a widespread assumption that whatever occurs "inside my head," so to speak, is necessarily subjective. In other words, because the divine dimension is an "inner" experience, it does not follow that it could not refer to something ontologically objective beyond the finite self. James takes quite seriously the mystics' feeling that invasions from the sub-conscious region suggest an <u>external</u> source for this feeling. James also takes seriously the possibility that mystical experience opens up a new dimension of fact to us. This is the contribution which empirical theology must make--to take religious experience as something more than simply aberrant psychological phenomena.

James goes even further and implies that the hypothesis of a divine agency, if it is taken seriously, must really make some significant differences in experience.[4] In other words he implies that there should be some verifiable consequences to the religious hypothesis. Unfortunately James's notion of verification is frightfully vague and totally psychologistic--involving differences that the belief in God would make to a person's life. In the light of contemporary concepts of what is required of verification, one would have to say that verification is not applicable to a religious hypothesis. This is why I say that epistemically, the most that religious experience can do is to suggest or give what I call <u>intimations</u> of divinity. To make stronger epistemological claims from an empiricist base seems to be unjustifiable. If the most that we can get from experience, however, are intimations of divinity, they are still intimations of an objective consciousness which exists, and James is to be commended for not fudging on this point. Religious experience points towards what may be taken as a genuine divine element of reality.

It is precisely at this point that empirical theology needs supplementation by both faith and reason; by faith, for genuine religion commits itself to much more than simply intimations of the divine; by reason, because once one has entered the circle of faith, one must consider the question as to which concept of divinity most adequately coheres with our experience and with our religious yearning. James begins but does not complete this task. What this involves, of course, is not an exclusive reliance on experience, for, as we have seen, God's peculiar modal status requires a rational development which goes beyond the bounds of experience, even interpreting it in its broadest Jamesian terms.

Empirical theology is the only link where discussion between the man of faith and the man who lacks faith can occur. James' "The Will to Believe"[5] is a classic case in point. In this grossly misunderstood article James does not try to prove something to the nonbeliever. He sets out certain factors in his own experience which might be common to the experience of others and indicates an option of the right to believe. James later regretted that he had not given this title to the article as it would have led to less misunderstanding of his position. In his article, "The Sentiment of Rationality,"[6] James talks of the sentiment as a common human urge for things to make sense. Here he takes a factor common in much human experience and tries to indicate why this might give us what I call _intimations of divinity_. The best religious philosophy is of this kind. In the _Phaedo_, Plato indicates common human experiences which point towards an element of radical transcendence in man--things in human life that point beyond pure animal existence and towards a spiritual dimension to experience. Kant says that if the purpose of human existence were simply to provide happiness, the universe did a poor job of it, intimating that perhaps human existence has other purposes than happiness. These are the kinds of things that I mean by intimations of divinity--intimations, because there is no attempt to prove God, but simply indications from human experience that a divine element might be present. They remain as no more than intimations unless and until one is touched by direct experience of the divine.

Empirical theism at its best is of this nature and should not be dismissed. It may help begin the process of religious exploration and it always serves as the foundation for later theological explication. In the beginning of this chapter we saw why it was not adequate as the last word in theism. Nevertheless, if theism, when launched, cuts off its empirical base and tries to maintain itself in a purely rational or revealed way, it can lead to patent absurdities. Only if one ignored experience could one come up with the peculiar doctrine of God's complete immutability to change and omnipotence in every respect. The doctrine of complete immutability makes nonsense of prayer life, divine response and religious experience, and the doctrine of absolute omnipotence makes a rational solution of the problem of evil impossible. Dipolar theism takes experience into account again and gives us a more intelligible doctrine of divine immutability and omnipotence than the doctrines that ignore experience. Thus, in this type of approach the insights of Augustinian theology cohere with experience instead of blatantly clashing against it. Even if inadequate in the end, James' doctrine of a finite God is also an attempt to make his intimations of divinity cohere with experience. This does not necessarily make his view true. Many think that he paid too high a price and I agree. Whitehead and Hartshorne provide a more adequate accommodation to experience than James at this point. Instead of simply opting for a finite God, a solution which has difficulties of its own, dipolar theism makes more rational and empirical sense by dividing God's nature into two aspects--an eternal and immutable aspect and a changing one. Thus, it is more coherent to have a God who is finite-infinite than simply a finite God. While the Whiteheadean view is more adequate than that of James, all of these views are in the tradition of empirical theology. Whitehead and Hartshorne are superior to James on this point because the two former thinkers take into consideration God's unique status. James' finite God would be another case of a contingent superior being C, of whom we spoke earlier. To preserve the insight that God must be in a special category and yet at the same time not desert the empirical foundation for theism, the dipolar view is much superior to a purely finite Jamesian deity. God is absolute and eternal in his primordial nature but empirical with contingent aspects in his consequent nature.

There is a further crucial point on which James and the view of dipolar theism agree and which is a major departure from orthodoxy. This is that God is genuinely limited in power over the world. In the orthodox view God is limited only by the logically absurd. For James, God is clearly a contingent being among other contingent beings in a pluralistic universe which is open and growing. For Whitehead, God and the world mutually require each other: no world, no God; no God, no world. God operates as a "lure for feeling," who by persuasion presents possibilities to actual occasions. In Whitehead's view God does not <u>give</u> freedom to man and to the created world; God's control over the world is limited essentially even though he is absolute and eternal in certain aspects. Hartshorne seems committed to the same view, though I have the impression that he would like to hold a position closer to orthodoxy on this point. It would seem that any coherent theistic view would have to opt for an essentially finite aspect of God in order to make sense of the problem of evil. We will look at this issue in more detail later in this study.[7]

What seems needed is the thorough grounding of theology and philosophy of religion in religious experience, no matter how vague and amorphous this may be. Otherwise theology becomes simply a logical exercise in dogmatism. Thus, empirical theology is an essential aspect in any adequate religious view; however, supplementation and "filling out" by reason and possibly by revelation is necessary. I say _possibly_ revelation, but I want to leave the question of revealed truth aside because recourse to such truth falls outside the bounds of philosophical justification, and it is only the latter with which I am dealing. The use of reason as applied to theistic doctrine falls well within the purview of philosophical discussion. From the intimations of divinity from all times and places and from the more dramatic kinds of religious experiences, we are encouraged to try to explicate a rational doctrine of the divine which will be true to our deepest religious insights and, thus, coherent with experience. While the concept of the divine is grounded in experience, our deepest insights seem to indicate that the divine falls under a special category and is not to be identified with any ordinary contingent being or beings. A not only unsurpassed, but an unsurpassable source of value is indeed something special.

NOTES

[1] For a major elucidation of Charles Hartshorne's views the following works are crucial: Man's Vision of God (Hamden, Conn: Archon Books, 1964); The Divine Relativity (New Haven: Yale U. Press, 1948); The Logic of Perfection and Other Essays in Neoclassical Metaphysics (LaSalle, IL: Open Court, 1962).

[2] William James, The Varieties of Religious Experience (New York: Longmans, Green and Co., 1935) pp. 485-520.

[3] William James, Essays in Pragmatism (New York: Hafner Publishing Company, 1948) p. 125.

[4] Ibid., p. 136.

[5] Ibid., pp. 88-110.

[6] Ibid., pp. 3-37.

[7] See Chapter 8.

CHAPTER 4

THINGS, PERSONS AND GOD: A PHENOMENOLOGICAL CONTRAST

Let us now move into the area of phenomenology, comparing our experience of things, persons and God in phenomenological terms, hoping thereby to show some interesting features that will emerge from such an inquiry. J. N. Findlay has provided a profound insight into our experiences of material objects:

> The object that is to be independent of ourselves must be subject to unalterable but discoverable laws, must fulfill the general expectation of behaving in a manner that we can learn to expect. Matter, bodies, have, in short, the sort of independence of our minds that two quarrelsome lovers have with one another: each feels bound to go against the other, and so in a sense to fulfill the expectations and ultimately the profound needs of the other. Matter would be truly independent of the mind only if its ways were so utterly confusing that we could never make head or tail of them. Whereas its role seems to be to tease, frustrate and ultimately to satisfy.[1]

Our experience of the external world is in many ways a matter of being teased, frustrated and then led on to satisfaction. Were experience too chaotic, we could not plan or predict; we could only watch and wait to see what would happen. Were experience too regular and lawlike, we could again do no more than observe ironclad necessities that occur. But in the world as it is we act. Such action can make sense only if the world partially frustrates and partially satisfies our desires and needs. To the extent that we can make some sense out of our material environment, there seems to be an affinity between matter and mind, but that affinity is limited because our knowledge always runs up against the unexpected and the frustrating.

Further to elucidate Findlay we may turn to C. S. Peirce's categories of <u>Secondness</u> and <u>Thirdness</u>.[2] Peirce maintains a direct givenness about objects. They present themselves to us as alien and distinct. We encounter them. We come up against them. In being other, they are resistant and recalcitrant--Peirce's category of Secondness. There is myself, and there is the datum of experience; hence the dyadic relation of Secondness.

Once we learn something about how these objects are likely to behave, at least to some degree, they cease to frustrate us and become instruments for our action. To act, however, we must have knowledge. This involves ability to predict, relying on lawlike development--Peirce's category of Thirdness. Knowledge of predictable law means going beyond what is simply observed; it involves an interpreter taking something as a sign of something else; hence the triadic relation of Thirdness.

Phenomenologically, our experience of things is a given whole in which both Secondness and Thirdness are present. For example, on attempting to emerge from some English railway carriages we meet obdurate resistance (Secondness) when we find no latch handle on the inside. Lack of knowledge produces frustration, but by assuming that carriage doors were made to be opened, we can discover elements of Thirdness or rationality. Law, order and an end of frustration ensue when we realize that we must push down the window and reach the latch from the outside. This exemplifies the dual nature of objects as being both open to and resistant to our expectations. When we know what to expect, prediction of real possibilities becomes feasible; that is, the element of Thirdness arises when we master the laws of an object.

In terms of our experience of things, the categories of Secondness and Thirdness seem to be crucial; Firstness seems less important. Peirce speaks of Firstness as sheer qualitative immediacy and also as the realm of the possible. Of course, a pure quality, like redness, taken in itself, can be only a possibility, because any actual quality is always given in a context, thus involving Secondness. Although Peirce applies Firstness to aesthetic immediacy, because such immediacy is independent of a larger context, this category seems to designate an abstraction rather than something concrete. Therefore, in discussing our experience, Secondness and Thirdness are more important than Firstness. I propose to examine the Phenomenology of things, persons and God in terms of these two categories. Things are both surprising and dependable at the same time. Even when we think we know what to expect we must still wait and see what will happen. This insight is the strength of all empiricisms and the downfall of all rationalisms. There is a kind of absurdity in what is given in experience that Sartre and others have graphically depicted. No principle of sufficient reason can be given as to why there should be anything at all rather than nothing. Epistemologically speaking, this is where we start, and this is where we end; but even to speak of givenness alone without the element of rationality is to speak in terms of abstractions, for in concrete experience, otherness is combined with the familiarity of order, confirmed expectation and law.

No physical object is completely alien to us; we can always classify it as "something" or other, even if we don't know what else to do with it. Most of the time we can do better. A bed, a chair or a table not only confronts us, it usually "behaves' as we expect that it will. We sit in a chair fully expecting it to sustain our weight and not suddenly to turn into a boa constrictor and choke us to death. Chairs never turn into boa constrictors, although they have been known to collapse when sat upon. This is where the element of law and rationality enters: Our experience of objects is generally dependable, but the surprising and unexpected can happen within a larger framework of order.

While the element of the surprising can always enter, the lawlike behavior of things is greater than that of persons. While we come up against both things and persons (Secondness), objects have a greater degree of Thirdness than persons--that is to say, things are more predictable in principle than persons. This is because things don't act, and action adds an element of the unpredictable. Animals are somewhere between things and persons in this regard. Things may be very complex and their laws difficult to uncover, but once the laws are discovered prediction is highly accurate. Persons are predictable too, but to varying degrees, and the possibilities of creative human action are a constant nightmare to social scientists who try to think of human behavior as analogous to things. In its simplest terms, a chair doesn't "do" anything, it just "is." A person "is," but even if his behavior is predictable to a high degree, one may always be thrown off guard because a person acts as well. In short, we might say that while Secondness and Thirdness are equally predominant features in things, the element of Thirdness is considerably reduced in regard to persons when compared to things. This is not to deny that actions can be brought under some lawlike relation once they have occurred, but we never know quite what a person will do next, whereas it makes no sense to wonder what a chair will do next.

Certain epistemological theories have tended to embrace one aspect or other of experience and to give it primacy. Much classical epistemology in the West has stressed the otherness of things, and frequently the gap between self and the world has been so emphasized that direct knowledge of an external world has been made impossible. We have only to think of the dualism of Descartes or of Locke's representative theory of perception. To stress the aspect of otherness alone is indeed to sunder knower and known so radically that genuine knowledge becomes all but impossible. On the other hand, certain other epistemological theories, generally associated with the temperament of the mystic, stress the unity of mind with the world to such an extent that there is no way to account for error, for action or even for experience as we know it. The mystic is overpowered by his desire for unity and completeness. He longs for the world to answer affirmatively his deepest human needs, and he wishes for complete fulfillment. Yet such fulfillment would make all action pointless because the self would merge with the world and there would be nothing for action to act upon. On a philosophical level this complete unity and intelligibility has been the goal of rationalism.

Besides obdurate givenness, what is most significant about our experience of objects is reliability. A world in which literally anything might happen next would scarcely be what we could call a world. The very idea of surprise would make no sense at all unless it were seen against a background of what is familiar. Thus, if everything were a surprise nothing would be a surprise, and the world would cease to have meaning. In discussing the problem of induction, philosophers have shown their awareness of the significance of reliability in human experience, but the relative unreliability of some types of human experience--particularly the religious--demands consideration.

When one compares religious experience with our ordinary experience of everyday objects, the interesting thing phenomenologically is the marked increase in the element of surprise and unpredictability. Peirce's categories of

Secondness and Thirdness, although not evenly balanced in ordinary experience, occur together frequently enough that we can function in an orderly world. In the area of religious experience Thirdness is diminished, and Secondness is more marked. A mystic may speak of religious experience in terms of the qualitative immediacy of Firstness, but until the mystic's ego disappears, religious experience _must appear to him_; thus, Secondness remains paramount.

The doctrine of God's grace represents a clear insight into the Secondness of much religious experience. We have tried to bring as much order into religious experience as we have done in other areas of experience, but without success. Elaborate techniques have been developed over the centuries in all religious traditions, attempting to assure direct experience of the divine or lawlike relationship to God. But at most such techniques can only set up what are hoped to be favorable conditions; they cannot guarantee success. Even the mystic who trains and disciplines himself recognizes that he must go through the "dark night of the soul." We cannot guarantee the presence of God, and we are often poignantly aware of his absence.

Those who demand complete reliability in religion do not know what they are asking for. The divine element is more like a person than like a thing. The demand for complete predictability in religion is the attempt to make God a thing after all. Things, while exemplifying Secondness, are more amenable to Thirdness. Persons are amenable to lawlike treatment and prediction too, but not to the degree to which things are. In fact the more predictable any person becomes, the more he is regarded as a <u>thing</u> and less as a person. Thus, although law and givenness are both present in regard to persons, the element of the unpredictable and the surprising is a peculiar feature of what it is to be a person. It is, thus, a major religious insight to realize that personhood is crucial to divinity.

There is, however, a sense in which the divine is less than person as well, and this has been a source of acute embarrassment to many religious people. The divine element not only seems to lack the predictability of things, it even lacks the predictability of persons. A thing has static givenness against a background of more or less reliable and predictable character. Normal persons can be capricious, creative, and surprising in a way in which things are not. But God's action is even more surprising and unpredictable than that of persons. In the experience of many people, God appears as Second, not as Third; thus, he seems too disorganized to be a person. It is true that there are many who seem to be constantly aware of the presence of God, but I expect there are many more to whom absence and frustration in the religious dimension is the norm. One might maintain that God is too well hidden to be a person. Divine givenness is rare enough that it is quite reasonable to call into question the very reality of the divine. Of course, there is much hiddenness in personality, but there is enough that is open and obvious that there is no problem about the existence of people the way there is about the existence of God. If ordinary matter teases, frustrates and satisfies us, as Findlay says, the element of elusiveness and teasing is even more marked in religious experience, and when satisfaction comes, its intensity and quality often seem greatly to exceed that made possible either by material objects or by persons.[3]

If ordinary experience were as disorderly and various in content as religious experience, we would not have a unified world but as many "worlds" as there are experiencing beings. Although we all view the world differently, most of us think of ourselves as inhabiting a common world, due to the givenness and the lawlike character of ordinary experience. But with religious experience there are many viewpoints with no common epistemological groundwork in terms either of givenness or of law to provide strong justification for our religious claims. This philosophic issue is at the heart of philosophy of religion: the lack of epistemic force for religious claims to knowledge and significance. Of course, many have pointed out that belief in the divine element is more a matter of faith than of knowledge, but the logical issue involved with epistemic force has not been stated as clearly as it should be. There is enough givenness in the divine dimension of experience to make sensitive and acute observers think there is something to religion after all, but there is so little more in terms of what reasonable men would expect that the "tough minded" are quite rational in rejecting the religious dimension as providing any insight into the nature of the real unless it is an insight into the peculiar psychology of the person having the religious experience.

An assumption frequently made is that failure to apprehend God is due to a willful refusal on the part of a person to open himself to the experience of God which is constantly surrounding him. The situation is often treated as analogous to refusing to admit that a chair exists because a person will not open his eyes and look. This attitude represents a failure to appreciate the significant difference between religious and non-religious experience and an attempt to subsume the former under the latter. It would be absurd to deny that there are willful turnings away from God, but on the other hand many people earnestly search and hope for this experience to become apparent to them without success. There are also many cases where the divine dimension breaks in unawares, in the absence of preparation, even to one who has a predilection against the religious.

Much experience of God is so capricious that the religious believer who is also philosophically acute must remain in some doubt about the authenticity of such experiences. Like his non-philosophical brother he must "wait upon the Lord." Unlike his fellow-believer, the philosopher will be struck by the oddity of the situation. What is also suggested by this discussion is that both Secondness and Thirdness are major criteria for determining what exists and is real, and where either factor is weak, puzzlement ensues about the existence and reality of what is involved. Phenomenologically, Secondness is crucial, but in the area of ontological commitment, Secondness is not a sufficient condition for determining that something <u>exists</u> and is real. "Existence" is well chosen to represent Secondness for it means to "stand out from," to be opposed to, or to confront. For existence and reality in the full sense we must combine this quality with Thirdness. A dream exists, but it exists as a dream; it represents a case of Secondness but only minimal Thirdness. Of course we might ask how it is possible to tell that something exists independently of the act of awareness. At this point Thirdness is crucial. We say that a thing exists and is real if its appearance and reappearance in a public manner is predictable and coheres with the surrounding environment and its lawlike order.

Precisely at this point the reality of God becomes problematic. From what has been said it would seem that even if we want to maintain that God exists, he does not seem to be real in what I have called the full sense of that term. He is not as real as persons and things because he does not exemplify lawlike behavior. This is a strange conclusion when one compares it with what theologians and philosophers down the ages have said. It has been traditionally maintained that God is that being which exists most fully of all, that he is indeed the paradigm of what it is to exist and to be real, and that all other existence is derivative from him. But in analyzing experience the situation is as I have described it.

If we go from the rarefied atmosphere of traditional theology to the modern consciousness of large numbers of persons, the feeling of the irrelevance and the unreality of God seems even more striking. We have only to look at twentieth century literature and philosophy to have this point brought home in striking fashion. The mystic analyzes his experience in a different way. He is so impressed with the impact, the Secondness, of the experience, that he maintains that God exists more fully than do things and persons. To read devotional literature is to realize that the impact of the divine experience, when it occurs, often far exceeds in force the impact of things and persons on consciousness. In fact the divine impact is often so extreme that it is reported to blot out ordinary consciousness of sensory objects just as the sun at daylight blots out the sight of the stars. Where one judges ontological commitment in terms of Secondness alone, God will, of course, be seen to have superior existential status to that of ordinary objects, as far as many mystics are concerned.

But the embarrassment for the religiously oriented epistemologist remains. Secondness alone will not do. After all, dreams and nightmares can have tremendous impact and blot out awareness of ordinary objects, but they do not represent real objects and states of affairs. From the other side of the fence, laws, while they are real, do not "exist" in Peirce's sense for while possessing Thirdness, they lack Secondness. Thus, <u>things and persons would represent the paradigm of what</u>

it is to exist and to be real. I hasten to add, that "reality" and "existence" are not coextensive terms. Much that does exist can be real, and something may exist without being fully real. What Peirce means here is that a law, such as the law of gravity, for instance, is not a "thing" that you could stumble across in the world. A "thing" is something you can collide with or come across directly in your path so to speak. A law is not this kind of entity, but it can be perfectly real nonetheless. The law of gravity is a real aspect of the world, but it is not a "thing" or event. An instance of the law, such as my falling off a log, is an existent event, exemplifying the law of gravity. On the other hand an event may exist but not be fully real for Peirce. For example, a dream of mine can exist or occur, but may not be subsumable under any known lawlike pattern of reoccurence. Hence it would not be fully real. Here I follow Peirce's realism in regard to law. An instance of a law exists, but this is something quite different from the law itself. The embarrassment of our epistemological claims concerning God is the absence of lawlike behavior in the dimension of the divine experience. This is why it will always make perfectly good sense to say that God is not real; yet many of us want to say that God exists and is real nevertheless.[4]

Everything in my analysis so far would suggest that one should not say that God is real in the full sense of the term. Yet one abandons religious consciousness altogether if one posits only a dreamlike existence for the divine. In terms of an epistemological analysis one must stop here, but precisely at this point the element of faith enters. This is nothing new. I am putting old truisms in the new garb of this kind of analysis to bring out the epistemological situation more clearly. There simply is a gap; all attempts to demonstrate that God is fully real must break down. The impact of awareness of the divine makes us think we encounter an "other," but the element of faith is required if we are to pass beyond the area of regarding the "other" as an element in our dream life. When the absence of God is apparent, all we can do is hope that his presence will manifest itself again in the future event of Secondness. But this hope must be an act of faith because our experience of God frequently lacks the connective link of Thirdness which is present in our experience of things and persons. Yet even here Thirdness may not be completely absent; such traits as goodness and love often appear and reappear in the encounter of man with God. Perhaps the categories are hidden because we only "see through a glass darkly."

NOTES

[1] J.N. Findlay, *The Discipline of the Cave* (London: George Allen & Unwin, 1966) p. 157.

[2] Charles Hartshorne and Paul Weiss, eds., *Collected Papers of Charles Sanders Peirce* (Cambridge, MA: Harvard University Press, 1960) 1. 300, 353.

[3] Here I am treating the phenomenology of those who experience the Divine as a *special* dimension of experience. Others may treat the religious simply as a heightened intensity of ordinary experience, including the vividness produced by drugs.

[4] In Chapter 5 we will examine those who *do* experience God in the mode of Thirdness. That many experience God as Third does not invalidate the findings of this chapter.

CHAPTER 5

GOD: FROM EXPERIENCE TO INFERENCE

In the previous chapter we examined one aspect of the human encounter or lack of encounter with God in phenomenological terms. We arrived at the disconcerting conclusion that as far as the experience of many persons (but by no means all) was concerned, the divine experience was capricious and irregular, lacking the features of lawlike predictability which characterize our experience of things and persons. Taking it at the phenomenological level, I would count an experience of God to be one in which a person sincerely reported that he had such an experience. Of course the hard philosophical question is whether the report of such an experience can be taken as a sign of a divine dimension to reality, which takes us into the question of inference which I shall treat later. At the moment I am concerned with bringing out some interesting features of the God-man encounter at the purely phenomenological level.

As we have seen, for many people in the modern world the God-man encounter does not occur at all, or only rarely and with different degrees of intensity, and the occurrences are unpredictable and capricious. To some degree this is to be expected if God is analogous to a person. The more lawlike and predictable a phenomenon, the more unlike a person it becomes. Thus, the most successful application of laws is to things, with considerably less success when it comes to persons--witness the difficulties in working out a scientific method for the social sciences. Thus, if God is to be conceived as in any sense personal, then a certain amount of capriciousness follows as a matter of course. For many, however, the experience of God is so capricious, so shrouded in mystery and so infrequent that it seems reasonable to doubt that there is a divine component at all. It was suggested that in such a situation, for many persons, faith was the intervening bridge between the rare occurrences of the divine-human encounter, which takes the place of the lawlike expectations that we have in regard to things and persons. For an increasing number of persons, of course, there seems to be no God-man encounter at all.

Before I run the risk of trying to draw some tentative philosophical conclusions, we must sketch in the phenomenological picture in more detail. Most people who consider themselves religious are not mystics; many are devout and true believers, but have rarely or never had what they call a divine-human encounter. Of course, this is not a matter of all or nothing. There are all degrees of what Otto calls the "numinous" in experience, which makes a phenomenological discussion on this issue all the more difficult. Much discussion, including my own, may leave the impression that there is a sharp dualism in experience between the secular and the religious, and in the religious you have what are clearly labeled mystical experiences of God. Now obviously there are such clearly identifiable experiences, and James and others have dealt with them extensively. Just because at one end of the spectrum we have experiences which seem clearly secular while at the other we have experiences that are religious, we should not fail to realize the vast continuum of experiences in between in which clear labeling in one category or the other would be a mistake. Anyone who takes theism seriously must maintain that in some sense God is pervasive in all experience (e.g., Whitehead), but it is only when experience reaches a peculiar level of value intensity that one takes it to be a religious experience of some kind. Seeking to remain at the phenomenological level, we could say, borrowing from James's account, that an experience gets classified as religious or as being an experience of Divinity when the person feels that his consciousness, and in particular his awareness of value, is continuous with a larger center of consciousness and value, not taken to be reducible to the value apprehension of other persons or of society, though it might be inclusive of these.

I certainly would not be foolhardy enough to propound this as a definition of religious experience. I am simply trying to suggest some kind of phenomenological schema into which it might be convenient to classify dimensions of experience which are taken to be of religious significance, or which are taken to involve a divine-human encounter. Even if one regards God's presence as pervasive throughout the world, it would not be conducive to philosophical clarity to call all experience religious, except in the sense just indicated that

God is ubiquitous. With this kind of schema in mind most of our experience would not be religious or mystical at all. Even our experience of shared value with other persons or with society would not necessarily be religious. Deep love between persons would not be religious per se. I want to suggest that one would begin to approach the religious dimension when he starts to take this union of one person with another as a manifestation or sign of a more basic union of self with environment. At this level, any religious dimension that enters would be mainly at the level of interpretation on the part of the person, of an experience which in its ordinary mode would not be thought to have any religious significance at all.

The same situation would hold in varying degrees of our enjoyment of natural beauty. For many people there is great value and intense enjoyment in the beauties of nature and many accept that experience on its own terms. The values enjoyed by the sportsman and the conservationist would not generally be taken to have any religious import. Such experiences are accepted for what they are and simply enjoyed. But when a person like Wordsworth begins to talk about the "brooding presence of the hills" and about the "presence that disturbs me with the joy of elevated thoughts," then he is beginning to take this experience as a sign of a continuous center of value. The universe itself begins to take on value properties and one is beginning to enter the domain of the religious. And from this one can go on to examples of the more dramatic and awesome confrontations that are reported in religious literature, such experiences as Moses and the burning bush or of Saint Paul on the road to Damascus. One can, of course, also examine the wealth of mystical literature where the numinous and awesome character of the experience makes one feel that he has confronted the living God.

With increasing numbers of persons in the modern world the divine dimension of experience is totally absent or is so infrequent and minimal as to be hardly worthy of notice. Large numbers of persons do not feel that human values and human needs for love and communion meet with any response beyond that of other men in society. It may be felt that man can achieve a modicum of communion with other men, but that the universe stands as obdurate and value-neutral. One might call this a humanistic view-point--that is, the only centers of values are human beings and the higher animals. These creatures can respond to each other, but beyond this there is simply the value-neutral world. Among those who would generally consider themselves to be at least conventionally religious, large numbers would rarely have what they would call a divine-human encounter, and for large numbers of persons religious experience is not essential at all. What is meant by adherence to a religion for these people involves propositional assent to dogmas and creeds of one kind or another plus faith.

There is another segment of the religious community whose importance cannot be overlooked, that segment which phenomenologically seems to more or less constantly have a sense of the presence of God, to be borne up by "the everlasting arms," the people who find God to be "closer than hands and feet." Among these people there is a dependability and lawlike reliance on the presence of God which to them makes God as actual and as real, if not more so, than is the case with persons. For these people God manifests all three of Peirce's categories, qualitative immediacy, confrontation with God as other, and a more or less continuing dependable relationship with the divine.[1] This is not to say that in such experiences God would never be absent or that the lawlike character of God's appearance would be ironclad--if such were the case God would <u>be</u> thing rather than person. But it is the case that to many religious believers, a sense of the more or less continuing presence of God, as a quiet background to their experience, is a more or less constant presence, providing strength, hope and creativity. From the religious perspective this is a "consummation devoutly to be wished." For these people doubts about the existence of God or of the importance of religion would seem minimal, for in such contexts God would be as "obvious" as things and persons, though in his own peculiar way. In this kind of situation there is an almost continuous sense of presence and continuity with a larger source of values than the self. While the interpretation of this experience will tend to be in the socially learned religious categories of the believer, at the phenomenological level people in this situation seem to have a sense of constancy and continuity with a center of value transcendent of themselves and of other persons. It is difficult again to know how to describe it, but many western theists refer to it as a sense of the presence of God.

Using Peirce's categories to elucidate this situation, though possibly not in a way he would subscribe to, we can say that for the persons we are considering now, God confronts the believer as an other--the category of Secondness, but mixed with this may be a large element of Thirdness. Such people, judging from their own reports, do not always have what James called "mountain top experiences" involving dramatic confrontations with the divine, though these do occur. One has only to consult various mystical writings to find many accounts of divine Secondness. Indeed, direct encounter with God is often taken to be the paradigm case of what a religious experience is all about. Much more frequent, however, may be the quiet undergirding of faith--gentle, hidden but pervasive, like trust or a sense of security. If this peculiar sense of presence is continuous and is relied on, it would seem that we have God in something similar to the mode of Peirce's Thirdness.

I argued earlier that our experience of persons appears in both the mode of Secondness and Thirdness; we confront them and in varying degrees we can rely on them and predict their appearances and behaviour. I also argued that while divine Secondness occurred, for large numbers of persons divine Thirdness was absent--that God's grace struck according to no known laws and that when it came to experience of God, the element of chance and unpredictability was paramount. The thesis is essentially correct as applied to large numbers of people, but in the group we are considering now, the element of divine Thirdness becomes marked, so that God, like persons, is existent and real. To the extent to which people feel they can rely and depend on the divine, the element of Thirdness is present. This, of course, is a crucial feature for many religious believers. Peirce's distinctions may be too crude to account for what I can only speak of as the alternation between Secondness and Thirdness which seems to occur with many persons. I suspect that there are a large number of devout persons who would never presume to say that they had confronted God in the mode of Secondness. To them God is hidden, but he is there. For many, the waters of religious faith run very deep, giving the believer a sense of assurance and certainty. If one thinks of Secondness as direct presence and of Thirdness as reliability and assurance, then, for many, God would appear almost totally in the mode of Thirdness. Yet this account will not quite do, for in Peirce's terms, Thirdness refers to law, and while a law is not directly present but can be relied on, the trust that religious persons have in God is obviously quite different from belief in the law of gravity and implicit reliance on it in acting. Suggestive as Peirce's categories are, possibly one should leave them at this point and say that trust in God is more like trust in another person, whether he is present or absent, except that the terms should be reversed. Trust in God, or in the nature of the universe would be the paradigm case of trust of which trust in another person would be a finite example, for persons are not infinitely dependable, but God would be. Thus, there would be in some sense a lawlike character to God, just as there is a lawlike character to persons. This might well be the marked feature of the divine in the experience of the persons we are considering now.

To people whose experience is of this nature, the existence of God would be no more problematic than the existence of the external world and the existence of other persons. To persons in this situation, the fact that others would be skeptical or non-believers seems perverse and to evidence a lack of faith. But it is precisely my point that for many others, divine Thirdness is minimal or totally absent, among both those who would call themselves religious and those who would not. It is this situation which makes God's existence and reality problematic.

Before we leave the phenomenological level, it might pay us to look at the role of faith as used in its religious sense in these different modes. For those whose experience of God would seem to be absent in any mode, faith would seem to involve a combination of belief in certain propositions about God, together with expectation and hope of some divine-human encounter. To many what would be involved would be a dogged determination to hold on to religious beliefs no matter what, in spite of no evidence or in the face of negative evidence, e.g., Job. Of more interest to us may be the persons who feel that they have encountered the divine from time to time in what we are calling the mode of Secondness. Here faith may involve not only propositional beliefs, but hope and expectation that God will appear again. One cannot predict if and when God will appear, but the experience that one has had before sustains the believer and gives him encouragement. God, the transcendent, would be a marked feature of this kind of experience--God as an independent center of force with a life of his own. God may also be felt as alien and dangerous in this mode of experience. The important point to keep in mind is that in this situation, in terms of the experience of God, it would be undependable, lacking order and predictability. Here the absence of divine Thirdness might well make the thoughtful person have real doubts as to the reality of God. Faith would be the important cement needed to bridge the gaps between unlawlike occurrences of divine Secondness. In one way it would be analogous to having faith in a friend whom you don't quite trust or know too well. The belief that your friend will manifest certain dispositions from time to time would be a matter of hope and expectation rather than solid knowledge. Of course in other respects the analogy with faith in God will break down in crucial respects. Faith in another human being is faith in another finite center of psychic awareness like yourself, one who simply cannot be relied upon absolutely. Faith in another person represents a mixture of hope and love with often a large element of anxiety and doubt. For the believer, in the absence of divine Thirdness, faith too would involve hope, love and expectation; the element of full trust would also be apt to be present. God, being an infinite center of psychic awareness, would merit absolute trust--this trust given to anything less than God would be idolatry. Of course, in the absence of predictable and lawlike experiences, the believer may also feel doubt and anxiety, for religious belief does not necessarily entail the absence of doubt, but it would not be doubt like the kind you would have concerning whether your friend was going to pull a fast one on you or not--it would be doubt as to the very reality and existence of God.

It would seem that faith plays a particularly crucial role for the believer in the absence of divine Thirdness, for here faith would be the only factor which could sustain the religious attitude in the face of doubt and discouragement. Here one would find the tragic and sublime aspect of religious faith in the face of adversity, and I mean by faith a basic trust in the nature of the universe rather than a propositional assent to certain dogmas though the two may go together. This peculiar faith or trust would not necessarily involve the belief that all is going to go well or that the believer thinks that his prayers will be answered in ways which are more or less satisfying to himself. It is rather the sense of being sustained in hope and strength no matter what happens. This is the miracle of religious faith, that it occurs not only with the absence of divine Thirdness, but even in the absence of divine Secondness as well. Faith here involves a deep emotional commitment to fill the intervening gaps where Thirdness is absent.

Commitment plus something more is involved when we talk about faith in connection with the people who experience God in the mode of Thirdness, possibly mixed with Secondness. Even when God is not directly present in their experience, they are apt to feel an assurance of God's ubiquitous nature. But here the emotional impact of <u>reliability</u> is greater than on those who have faith in the sense of hope and expectation. God is present but absent at the same time in this kind of situation. He is present in the sense that the believer feels sustained and held up by "the everlasting arms." The assurance of God is not intermittent but a constant and pervasive backdrop to experience. It would be something like knowing that someone is in the house who cares, and yet he is in another room and you don't see him. The believer might report that he has a kind of haunting sense of presence and yet he might deny that he has any out-and-out divine-human encounter or the union with God in ecstacy which so many mystics talk about. This would not preclude the possibility of direct mystical encounters with God, but such encounters would not be essential. It is too bad that the dramatic mystical encounters are often taken as essential in order to be in the presence of the divine. Significant and valuable as that is when it occurs, probably much more usual is the "still small voice," the sense of the presence of God, quiet, gentle, non-compulsive, but there nevertheless, like the loved one in the next room. To call it Secondness seems inappropriate; to call it Thirdness seems inappropriate; it is both and neither, but it is a pervasive factor in the religious experience of many persons.

Up to this point, with some help from Peirce's categories, I have been indicating various types of experiences of the divine at the purely phenomenological level. I have tried to refrain from deriving any philosophical conclusions from the data. It might be of some interest now to make some tentative explorations in that direction. The varieties of religious experience indicate that any conclusions drawn must be of a most tentative character at best. It certainly doesn't take a survey to show that the existence of a divine component, let alone a personal God, is highly problematic. Our phenomenological study is an attempt to indicate some of the reasons for this. Where all three Peircean categories are more or less operative at the phenomenological level, we tend to accept the existence and reality of the phenomena under consideration. In this sense the reality and existence of things and persons is not problematic although there are, of course, many epistemological problems connected with our knowledge in these areas. In the case of experience of God, we found only one group of persons, admittedly a sizeable group, who experienced the divine in what one might call all three Peircean modes. A sizeable group seemed to experience the divine only intermittently in something like the mode of

Peircean Secondness, and a very large group had no experiences at all that it would classify as the divine in any mode whatsoever. I have not said much about the mode of divine Firstness because I am more interested in the questions of existence and reality and this is where Secondness and Thirdness are crucial, where one seeks to establish this.[2] The crucial drawback to making any ontological inferences is, of course, the lack of public verification. One does not have to be a positivist to realize that while things and persons can be made present to others, this is not true in the case of God. From this fact alone many empiricists will quite rationally give up the inquiry at this point; the phenomenological aspects we have outlined provide interesting data for a study of religious psychology and sociology, but ontologically and metaphysically nothing of interest follows. And yet the pervasiveness of the divine element in human experience past and present leaves many wondering if a genetic reductionism of the religious is an adequate response. With all this phenomenological smoke there just might be some ontological fire. And yet even with some tentative ontological explorations into this realm, we know that in the last analysis the issue will remain open, calling either for an act of faith or no such act.

At the philosophical level, our justifications for the epistemological claim that things and persons are existent and real involves appearance to a significant degree in each of the three Peircean modes plus some intersubjective testability. Thus the claim to know that there is a divine component which exists and is real, is to make a claim which cannot be rationally justified in the ordinary ways. This is not a particularly startling conclusion, but it is well to point out the logic of the situation in any case. Leaving aside the non-rational factors in religious belief, are there any rational considerations which might legitimately enter into the formation of religious belief?

The tentative conclusions I wish to suggest stem from the phenomenological analysis we have undertaken.[3] Beyond this there are a host of reasons which have been presented over the ages within natural theology, but I want to restrict myself to inferences made from the phenomenological base sketched here. The persistence of the religious dimension of experience in all ages and cultures is worth noting in this regard. In spite of various attempts at reductionism, the numinous and transcendent value character of experience is still quite widespread, even though there may be much more caution and hesitancy in drawing ontological conclusions from this experience than in the past. Still the persistence of this phenomenon in millions of people lends some credence to the idea that there is an encounter of man with some transcendent source of values.

Take the reports of the mystics in the mode of divine Firstness and Secondness. One comes up against a transcendent "other" which qualitatively is felt to be a source of value or a center of supreme value. Now there is a natural tendency to assume (and generally with good reason) that what occurs in one's consciousness is also objective. While consciousness is intentional and, thus, directed outward, the basic reason for assuming that our intentional acts are of an "object out there" is intersubjective testability. Yet while recognizing the lack of testability, many persons will take the brute Secondness of the divine-human encounter to indicate that what arises in consciousness as other, therefore, is ontologically transcendent of consciousness. There is a *prima facie* objectivity to whatever we confront, from the sheer fact of confrontation, a point which primitive mythological consciousness accepted, but which modern sophisticated persons do not. There are sound reasons for assuming that what occurs *outside the boundaries of our bodies* represents a confrontation with things, persons and events which have an ontological status which transcends our awareness of them, and for assuming that what *occurs only "within" the confines of our own bodies* is simply a manifestation of our own selfhood. Yet it may be a dogma of sophisticated twentieth century empiricism that *nothing* that seems to occur *only within the boundaries of our own skin can at the same time have ontological transcendence beyond the self*. This assumption, as Jung and others have pointed out, may have resulted in cutting modern man off from his psychic roots and given him the illusion that he is a completely self-contained organism, not rooted at all in a collective unconscious life. One does not have to accept Jung's theory or call for a return to primitive mythological consciousness to call this modern dogma into question. It may be that in the past when persons heard an inner voice they were too prone to externalize it as the voice of God, and certainly all kinds of weird experiences happen to people who are all too prone to attribute objective significance to these experiences, and no intelligent person would accept all these reports at face value. There is still a world of difference between the cautious willingness to allow that some inner occurrences may have ontological significance beyond the self and the outright denial that this is possible at all.

Some would argue that a confrontation of self with another _in_ one's own consciousness should never be taken as a confrontation of self with another _transcending_ consciousness unless public tests of externality can be applied. A kind of Occam's razor principle would be applied here enjoining one against making any ontological commitments unless forced to. Up to a point this is a very sound strategy for any position that purports to be empiricist and it would be rash indeed to go from something in consciousness directly to an ontological commitment outside of consciousness without further reason. But it is precisely the pervasive character of the religious consciousness that should at least make an empiricist admit the possibility that what is taken by many to be a divine-human encounter at the phenomenological level might also be a divine-human encounter at the ontological level. Beyond this the man of faith must go, but this is as far as an open-minded empiricist can go with reason.

The mystic, on the other hand, feels his consciousness confronting a larger center of value consciousness and passes easily from the phenomenological level to the natural attitude of ontological belief and experience of the divine. The mystic presumably does not make an <u>inference</u> from the experience to the being of the divine any more than the ordinary person makes an inference from chair-like sense data to the reality of a chair. Peircean Secondness precludes the necessity of <u>inferring</u> an outer referent from an inner experience. As many contemporary philosophers point out, we are already in the world, so there is not a problem of how to get there. The inferential component comes in interpreting the qualities of experience given as Seconds into the rational modes of Thirdness. The natural attitude is to accept the reality of whatever we experience unless our expectations are not fulfilled. The mythological mind of the primitive is much more liberal in his ontological commitments than is the sophisticated modern mind. The phenomenological attitude has to be consciously and deliberately developed--"bracketing" requires a peculiar act of abstraction. The mystic presumably has to make an <u>inference</u> as to the <u>nature</u> of the divine which he encounters, whereas the encounter simply occurs. Of course in all of our experience, including the religious, encounter and inference go together; the philosopher makes the separation for purposes of discussion.

The natural attitude in dealing with things and persons is to go from phenomenology immediately to ontology. In these situations it requires a special act of "bracketing" to drop the ontological commitment inherent in the natural attitude. In the case of the divine the natural attitude for many is also one of ontological acceptance, but for many others there is hesitancy and drawing back, or a refusal to connect the two to begin with.

When we confront a person or an object, we confront not only a public object but a sharply demarcated <u>object</u> with definite spatial boundaries. In the human-divine confrontation, an indeterminate and nebulous factor enters. The confrontation may be definite enough, but just what is confronted becomes more problematic. Confronting God is more like confronting a mood in another person, or coming into a room full of people and confronting an atmosphere. The confrontation or Secondness of the situation is definite enough, but it has no sharp spatial boundaries; there is no clearly definable object. And if another person present says "I don't see what's going on here," one is at a loss to know what to do. You can't say "Look, there it is" and point, as you can to a chair. A mood or an atmosphere can be perfectly real, transcending the consciousness of the individual person. The person who enters a subway car whose occupants are being entertained by a drunk immediately "senses" something on entering which is not usually present when he gets on the subway. The atmosphere is "there"; he didn't make it, but it doesn't make sense to apply literal spatial predicates to it, e.g., how wide is it? Of course, in the subway car, the atmosphere, while not dependent on one particular person, is a function of the drunk and of the other persons, and when the drunk leaves the atmosphere leaves too, so we attach no particular ontological significance to this.

However, I said our experience of God is <u>something like this</u> in the sense that the example is used to throw light on the divine-human encounter and to indicate certain similarities. The significant difference is that the religious believer thinks of God as transcendent of all acts of human awareness of him. Furthermore, a significant aspect of the divine-human encounter is the feeling that one is in contact with a source of superior value, or what one might call the sense of the <u>ideal</u>, either in the form of a value one aims at or of an obligation that one feels, often accompanied by feelings of radical guilt. Possibly the nearest that one might get to divine Thirdness would be in the area of the ideal. The ideal as moral, as love, as compassion may be a continuous feature of religious experience and also involve divine Firstness--the qualities of God.[4]

Widespread in religions both primitive and modern is the sense that one is in contact with a psychic center <u>superior</u> in some respect to the person. The superiority in question may be in the area of power, love or magic. What is interesting is that there seems to be generally a groping towards an ideal dimly apprehended but out of reach, and part of what we call the difference between primitive and more advanced religions lies in the demands put upon the ideal. For example, human consciousness comes to demand ethical predicates attached to the ideal. An ethically sensitive man becomes superior to a God of sheer power or magic manipulation. As human consciousness develops we come to demand more from our concepts of divinity, or one could say that we gain a deeper insight into the nature of the divine as human consciousness and awareness develop. God comes to be apprehended not so much as an egotistical grossly anthropomorphic power-mad superman, but as a vastly superior center of persuasive love and concern. We apprehend the God we are ready for--as our sensitivity increases further aspects of the divine are disclosed to us.

I am aware that from the data of the religious consciousness the philosophical interpretation can be taken in either direction. The increased subtleties that occur in our concepts of the divine may simply reflect the fact that man's psychic needs become more complex and, thus, he projects on to the external world more complex concepts of divinity to satisfy those needs, or they may reflect steadily deepening insights into the nature of a real divine component external in some sense to man and society. The latter interpretation runs more ontological risk and one cannot prove that it is so, but it could be so. Thus, such considerations stem from _intimations_ of divinity, and this is as far as rational and empirical considerations can take us in our ontological quest. What comes thereafter must be supplied by faith.

NOTES

[1] Charles Hartshorne and Paul Weiss, eds., Collected Papers of Charles Sanders Peirce (Cambridge, MA: Harvard University Press, 1960). See in particular 1. 300, 353.

[2] For further aspects of divine Firstness, see Chapter 6.

[3] Further conclusions will be drawn in Chapter 10 concerning ontological results drawn from a phenomenological base.

[4] See Chapter 6.

CHAPTER 6

DIVINE FIRSTNESS: THE QUALITATIVE APPROACH TO GOD

Since we have discussed the existence and reality of God in terms of Peirce's categories of Secondness and Thirdness, I now want to borrow Peirce's category of Firstness to throw light on a discussion of the <u>qualitative nature</u> of God.

As a phenomenological category, Firstness seems the most puzzling of the three. Compared to Firstness, Secondness and Thirdness seem relatively uncomplicated. The dyadic relation of reaction involves concrete individuals, while a law, though abstract, is real enough in its own terms. Firstness, on the other hand, seems to have aspects of both the concrete and the abstract. For Peirce, Firstness denotes <u>qualitative</u> immediacy--like a given shade of red, and also--possibility. There is a sense in which qualitative immediacy would be concrete, while a possibility would clearly seem to be an abstraction. The clue to the linking of the two is that for Peirce, both are <u>Firsts</u>. What this means specifically is that a given shade of red, <u>taken independently of anything else</u>, is a monadic predicate and thus a First. We have already seen that a possibility is abstract. There may be a sense in which qualitative immediacy is abstract too. In one sense a given shade of red would seem to be concrete, but taken as a monadic predicate, independent of everything else, it would be abstract. Any concrete actual shade of red, however, would have to be in a relation of Secondness to the larger context in which it is embedded; actual red must be a red something or other a sunset--a book, or a chair. Thus, a given shade of red taken as a monadic predicate is an abstraction. Peirce sees the three categories in terms of Possibility, Actuality and Law.

In any case I have borrowed Firstness here to emphasize that I am interested in qualitative nature as such, as applied to God. Thus, the problems that may arise with this category need be of no concern in this discussion. What is of concern is what one can say about God, given a general empiricist orientation. If "encounter with the divine" is taken phenomenologically as a mode of experience, what characterizes such experience?

I am interested in certain qualitative textures of experience which seem to be present in what many call awareness of the divine. These qualitative textures are widespread and are regarded as important by most sophisticated theists and by many other religious believers as well. The first such texture I would call the Ideal, taken primarily in the ethical sense. Part of what is involved here is that concepts of the divine are constantly outgrown--earlier concepts being found inadequate, being supplanted by others. It has been said that a little thinking takes you away from God, but more thinking brings you back. If you do come back, the final concept is not the beginning one. What is it in experience which makes people feel their concept of divinity is inadequate? What is it that makes some people "outgrow" a specific concept of God? A naturalistic rejoinder at this point might be that it is a mark of maturity to "outgrow" any concept of God whatsoever. It might be said that one no longer needs a concept of God at all. While this is certainly a reasonable response, one can also think of religious consciousness as a situation where one outgrows a concept of God because one seeks to find a more profound concept of the divine that will be adequate to the believer's religious experience. Why did the gods of ancient antiquity cease to fulfill the religious needs of people? For one thing, many people were morally superior to these gods. The gods were more powerful than mortals, but Socrates, Plato, and Aristotle so far outdistanced them in terms of moral character and in terms of the complexities of human personality that the ancient gods simply became religiously worthless. The notion of the Ideal indicated to sensitive ancients that something more is required of divinity than was to be found in the pantheon of gods.

In terms of qualitative immediacy, <u>power</u> has been an essential quality of divinity from the days of primitive animism to the present, but power alone can be demonic as well as divine. At the level of ethics, power per se is neutral. Certainly the lack of any power would make divinity radically deficient. Power may be a necessary but not a sufficient condition of divinity. The concept of power has been given undue prominence in the western theistic tradition, as Whitehead has pointed out. The ethical ideal has stimulated both the western and the eastern tradition to ask for something more than power--power tempered with mercy and love. As Whitehead has shown, God is much more profoundly apprehended through the qualities of persuasion and love than through that of sheer force or power.

At the phenomenological level <u>power</u> and <u>love</u> are seen as two major qualitative constituents of the divine. They have not usually been combined in a very coherent way, but many have found them to be important attributes of divinity. Frequently they have been combined in such a way as to make the concept of God self-contradictory or paradoxical. Within the orthodox Christian tradition, many have wondered how it is possible that God could exercise power and love by saving some and damning others to an eternal hell. There is a sense in which God would have to be powerful and a sense in which God is loving, but unless we give up the attempt to make intelligent sense out of theism altogether, these qualities must be combined in divinity in a way which makes sense. If one insists on no limits on divine power, then this would seem to rule out divine love, for love must be freely given and freely received or rejected. Any being who is open to giving and to receiving love must be limited in power in some sense, in that he simply cannot force love.

Traditional theists would prefer to say that God freely limits the exercise of his power rather than to say that God is really limited in power. I would prefer to say that the power is really limited in fact, for love cannot be coerced from a creature, even by God. Fear and obedience can be coerced but love is something else again. This appears to be a purely semantic difference, but I suspect more is involved here. While God could indeed withold the full exercise of his power, allowing love to develop, the point is that the love of the creature for God must develop of its own accord, if at all and in the last analysis there is a point beyond which God cannot go. Dipolar theism brings this out in stressing the pole of the finite in the infinite-finite being.

Dipolar theism shows a coherent way in which divine power and divine love can be combined. As religious consciousness develops, the divine comes to be seen as ethically surpassing in a supreme way the most saintly ethical humans. Another way of putting it is to say that anything that could be surpassed ethically by humans could not be God. As we saw earlier, while ethics can be treated independently of God and developed on an autonomous basis, many religious thinkers would argue that ultimately God's ethical qualities stand as the paradigm case of what it is to be ethical on the human level. Some would argue that unless we had some dim intimations of divinity, we wouldn't know what it was to be ethical.

Connected with this sense of the ethically ideal is man's sense of radical finitude and radical guilt. Describe it how you will, as humans we are deeply aware that our best efforts fall short of what they should be. In our dealings with others and, in particular, with those closest to us we know that no matter how hard we try we cannot love enough, cannot be responsive enough, that no matter what we do we will always be radically deficient in a profound sense. Some are more acutely conscious of this than others, but all of us are affected in some way at some time by this basic limitation in the human condition. Religious experience is not radically cut off from ordinary experience. All of us feel this limitation to varying degrees; those who feel it in a peculiarly acute form in terms of feelings of radical guilt will often tend to interpret this aspect of experience in religious terms. If there is anything to theism at all God must be pervasive in experience at all levels, but the divine dimension is only recognized as such when peculiar levels of intensity of experience are reached. In Kierkegaard the feeling of radical guilt is quite acute; in others, not so much.

Thus, in religious experience, no matter how dimly perceived, <u>power</u> and <u>the ethically supreme</u> stand out as qualities of divine Firstness--the <u>qualitative texture</u> of these experiences becomes apparent and our sense of radical guilt and deficiency becomes a Peircean Secondness to these qualities of Firstness against which we measure ourselves and are found wanting. Whether there is <u>in fact</u> a divine component or whether such experiences are simply a projection from human consciousness does not affect the phenomenological description. It is apparent once again that experience--any experience--is essentially ambiguous. It lends itself to multiple interpretation. Throughout this study it is clear that what is described can be taken either as divine disclosure or as psychological projection. The choice is always ours and experience per se does not force us into one option or the other.

Built into our idea of what it is to be human is the awareness that we could always be better than we are. Kant saw the point clearly in his contention that the only thing good without qualification was a good will--and the morally perfect will could reside only in God. Only in a divine will could inclination and duty coincide, that is to say, be completely congruent. As for humans, no matter how good they are, there is some lack of congruence between inclination and duty. We might say that all humans have some obligations--which is to say they have things they ought to do. God, being the perfectly good will, would have no obligations in this sense. Being imperfect, there are many things I know I ought to do which I do not do. For God, this situation could not arise because being a perfect will, what ought to be and what is would coincide. In other words "ought" involves imperfection because "ought" arises only where I <u>fail</u> to do something I ought to do. This would not apply to God. It is important to note for our purposes this ideal of moral perfection which is widespread in human consciousness as a phenomenological datum. To move directly from phenomenology to ontology at this point would be to construct a form of the moral argument for God's existence as used by some natural theologians. This sense of moral perfection occurs in human experience, but how experience is to be interpreted is open to choice. If one chooses to take this as an intimation of divinity (and epistemically one is scarcely justified in saying anything stronger), the sense of the morally perfect will could be considered a qualitative character of the divine in the mode of Peircean Firstness.

Many, particularly in the Judeo-Christian tradition, have considered power and moral perfection to be the most important attributes of divinity. Many think that a more important mode of divinity than either of these (though it does not rule these out) is _love_. This is a frightfully ambiguous term with a multiplicity of meanings, so let me approach love as a mode of divine Firstness by means of a method resembling Wittgenstein's idea of "family resemblance." There is not one unique aspect to love, but several important aspects which is why it may be of value to talk of a "family resemblance" of meanings. The first aspect of love I want to deal with is what we might call the _aesthetic_.

Under this term let us include two modes--that of _awareness_ plus that of _satisfaction_. This combines the archaic sense of the term, akin to Kant's usage, where the aesthetic is used for that which is apprehendable in experience with the more modern usage, related to the sense of beauty (aesthetic value in the modern sense). The most explicit use of the aesthetic in this sense occurs in Whitehead's thought where, as satisfaction or value, it is pervasive of his entire philosophical system. Hartshorne has pushed this characterization further, as applied to God, speaking of God as the paradigm case of the aesthetic--infinitely open to and aware of all that takes place and taking satisfaction in the entire created universe--thus divinity as expressed through love. Many, particularly in the west, experience God in the modes of power and ethical perfection, as we have already seen. When God tends to be apprehended exclusively in these modes, religious experience takes on a grimness and foreboding character that at its worst produces the strict literal moralism that one finds in Biblical fundamentalism, and possibly at its best in the radical guilt before God, associated with Kierkegaard. A theme which is not as dominant in our tradition, but which needs to be stressed more, is God experienced as enjoyable, and as the source of satisfaction. If God is experienced in the mode of guilt before judgment, God is also experienced as "the everlasting arms," as the still presence in the natural universe that Wordsworth speaks of. This qualitative character of the divine is extremely subtle and elusive. There is a pervasive feeling that many religious believers have, that at its base the universe is basically good, that it is joyful in the sense that value as satisfaction is operative throughout.

In its most developed form this is _not_ the feeling that God will answer my prayers, that all will work out for the good, that evil is not real but only an appearance. People who feel this way do apprehend God as the conserver of value, at least to some degree, but what I am concerned with is the feeling that in the profoundest sense the universe seeks the creation and enhancement of value in spite of the fact that God does not answer all prayers in an obvious way, that things do not always work out for the best and that evil is only too real. These feelings may express themselves in the more dramatic mystical feelings of oneness with all creation, but more frequent, I suspect, is the quiet sense of support of the "everlasting arms" and the feeling of the writer of the twenty-third Psalm that God is with him even in the "valley of the shadow of death."

What do we mean by the creation and enhancement of value? Here I would see value tied very closely to the aesthetic notion of satisfaction. Obviously I am very drawn to Whitehead's doctrine at this point where creativity is taken as a primitive, involving prehension of the past, the entertainment of possibilities and the satisfaction derived from creating something new in the present. The "root metaphor" of Whitehead's metaphysics is the notion of aesthetic satisfaction. If we were to move into an ontological and metaphysical direction at this point, the path that Whitehead has blazed would be an obvious one to follow. Metaphysically one might talk about <u>God's</u> satisfaction, but at the level of phenomenological description we must talk about <u>man's</u> satisfaction and sense of value apprehended by man. At one level human enjoyment of anything involves the two modes of the aesthetic of which I spoke earlier. To enjoy anything is to be aware of it and also to derive satisfaction from it. Enjoyment can cover anything from the invigorating feelings after a good swim to the most complex satisfactions involved in the performance and completion of creative work. In addition to individual enjoyments of this kind one can speak of a life enjoyable on the whole, which is something different from simply an additive sum of separate enjoyments. These are the intrinsic values--the ends for which extrinsic and instrumental values serve as means. The purpose of life as Lewis indicates is a life found satisfying in the living of it.[1]

Human satisfactions can be viewed in a non-religious way and naturalistic value theories such as those of Dewey and Lewis present a coherent picture of man as an active valuer in the world. Phenomenologically, humans act to achieve value--value is pervasive in human experience. Suppose, however, I choose to take this experience of value enjoyment as disclosure of the divine--as disclosure of the qualitative character of divinity. While the feeling of radical guilt is more frequently taken as divine disclosure, why should one not take enjoyment as disclosure as well? Proof? Argument? No. We are talking again about intimations of divinity. The epistemic force involved is tenuous and hidden, but I want to argue that it is not totally absent. When we feel most alive, when enjoyment pervades our soul and body, <u>we seem to feel part of a larger process of life</u>. This feeling is not necessarily consciously apprehended explicitly. Our enjoyment is directed outward to things and persons. But one can take these feelings as a sign of relation to a divine being possessing the qualities of the aesthetic.

Let us note that the sense of being aware and alive, satisfied by creative work and "in touch" with the surrounding environment can be taken as an intimation of divinity in the mode of Peircean Firstness. The feeling of basic well being, of what the young call "good vibes" is simply that and nothing more unless and until one wants to take them as intimations of divinity. We now have several qualitative characteristics of the divine--power, the ethically supreme, and love as awareness and satisfaction.

Let us look further at divine love in terms of certain "family resemblances." We have already spoken of love in terms of awareness and satisfaction. Another aspect of what could be taken as a manifestation of divine love is what, following the insight of Otto Friedrich Bollnow, we might call trust.[2] At the experiential level he speaks of it as a general trust in life, and maintains that this "trust in being" is an essential condition for human life. This is a profound insight and one that has been too often overlooked. This cosmic trust is not to be identified with a shallow optimism that everything will turn out for the best. It is a kind of "gut level" feeling, too deep for clear expression, that in some basic sense the universe can be relied on in the pursuit of one's activities. Part of it is reliance on the more or less lawlike structure of the universe, but I suspect that this is only a small part of it. It is the basic sense of hope in life that most of us maintain in varying degrees even in the face of extreme adversity. The other side of the coin is a kind of cosmic despair which Heidegger and other existentialists have stressed so much. As Bollnow has pointed out, existentialists have concentrated on despair with little attention to the other side of the coin--hope and trust.

One might argue the case that life, no matter how bad must have some degree of this cosmic hope and trust and that when it is absent completely, natural death or deliberate suicide is not long in coming. There are people who, in the profoundest sense, do not wish to live, and who seem to wither and die as a result. It is reasonable to suggest that this occurs when this basic trust is absent. One must stress that this trust is not focused on any particular object or event any more than Heidegger's despair has such a focus. This hope and trust is cosmic in its dimensions.

At the phenomenological level this trust is an interesting datum of human existence. This basic kind of belief in life, or better, feeling for life, seems essential in some degree for the sustenance and continuance of human existence, but at this level no implication is made that this trust in the universe is justified in any sense. Again we face a choice as to whether to take this datum of human experience as an intimation of the divine or not. If we do choose to so regard it, this deep feeling in human experience can be viewed as the source of the believer's feeling that God is trustworthy, and the ability to trust in the divine is seen as another aspect of divine love. God would be seen by many as the paradigm case of trustworthiness--that on which one can rely no matter what, not in the sense of getting whatever you want, not in the sense of a cosmic insurance company, but the paradigm case of what trust is. Thus, divine love as a quality of God would involve this aspect. The ability to love profoundly may open up to some humans dimensions of the universe that are closed to others. Bollnow, in his article, points out that Scheler was possibly the first to remark that certain ultimate experiences of being are only accessible to the man who loves.

Another aspect of the qualitative character of God, which has been thoroughly documented is God felt as the numinous, the mysterium tremendum, dealt with so well in Otto's classic work.[3] There are other aspects which we have not discussed[4] but enough has been said, I think, to indicate that much can be said about God as experienced in the mode of Peirce's Firstness.

NOTES

[1] C. I. Lewis, <u>An Analysis of Knowledge and Valuation</u> (La Salle, IL: Open Court, 1946).

[2] Otto Friedrich Bollnow, "The Conquest of Existentialism," <u>Universitas</u> Vol. 2, No. 2, 1958.

[3] Rudolf Otto, <u>The Idea of the Holy</u> (New York: Galaxy Books, 1958).

[4] God felt as threatening and demonic. What Whitehead refers to as "God the enemy." While these are important phenomenological aspects of our experience of God, they do not seem to be as basic as the ones I have mentioned. Otherwise, theistic belief would turn into demonology.

CHAPTER 7

GOD AS PERSON

In discussion of the qualitative character of God, many qualities have been attributed to him such as power, justice, love, goodness, etc. Perhaps the most important quality as far as western theism is concerned, is personhood. To many, the attribution of personhood to God seems anthropomorphism of the grossest kind--simply a primitive projection of human needs. Somebody said that if triangles could pray, God would be worshipped as a triangle. It would be foolish to be unaware of the Freudian critique where God is seen as a father image. It is also evident that there are many conceptions of God, subjective and immature in character, reflecting human wishes and childhood fantasies. The simplest thing would be to treat concepts of God as projections of human needs and as nothing more. Thus, from the crudest kind of anthropomorphism to the most sophisticated concept of the divine, we would be faced with simple wish fulfillment. Given such a situation what would be the point in talking about God as person at all?

If one chooses to read experience in this way it certainly can be done, but suppose within the context of the religious life one chooses to take the concept of God seriously and makes a detailed philosophical study of the issue. William James, though fully aware of the psychological motives behind religion, nevertheless treated religious knowledge claims fairly, without engaging in a facile reductionism.

If one is to consider God as person one has to face the charge of anthropomorphism--that man builds God in his own image. First of all it must be agreed that this is unavoidably true to some extent. A long tradition has recognized that talk of God is analogical in character. Unless we are to give up the attempt to talk about God at all, we can only refer to him in terms drawn from our own life and experience. Maybe the remark that to a triangle God would be triangular is not completely wrong. If a triangle could conceptualize, what else could it do but conceptualize in its own terms? If God is ubiquitous, all creatures of the universe would experience God in the way appropriate to the creature involved. Any creature can only experience the world in its own frame of reference, depending on what kind of creature it is. A plant can only experience the world as a plant, an animal can experience it only as an animal and man only as a man. If one translates this aspect of things to God does it mean that God is plant, animal and man all wrapped up in one? Most would say no. A corollary which follows immediately is that God cannot literally be a plant, an animal or a man, but this should not be too startling as it is doubtful that any talk about God is literal except possibly the assertion that he exists. While we cannot say that God is literally a plant, an animal or a person, we can say that God can only be experienced by each kind of creature in the way appropriate to that creature. If that is the case then the appropriate way for humans to experience God is God as person, which is not to say that God is _a_ person. Thus, anthropomorphism, in some sense, is unavoidable in talk about God, but the gross anthropomorphism which sees God as _a_ person can be rejected from the discussion at the outset. The importance of this distinction needs to be stressed and kept in mind. Legitimate anthropomorphism cannot avoid speaking of God _as_ person, but illegitimate anthropomorphism is involved when one speaks of God as _a_ person.

It might be said at this point that from the perspective of a dog, while it would be illegitimate to say God is a dog, it would be legitimate to speak of God as dog--and this seems very strange to say the least. If dogs could engage in theology, the only thing they could do would be to speak of God as dog, while denying that God is a dog. This peculiar example is worth looking at in some detail. Many religious thinkers have pointed out that God must be open to and aware of all creatures in the world--that without being a person God sympathizes with and is aware of what it means to be a person and suffers along with us in our sufferings. After all, what does the symbolism of the cross mean if not this? Looked at in this way, is it so strange that God would be aware of and know what it is to be a dog without being a dog himself? Is it so strange that God would know and be aware of what it is to be a plant, without being a plant himself? All of this seems to follow naturally if we maintain, as many have, that God is open to all, sympathetic with, and aware of all creatures--even though the creatures involved would seem to have no awareness of him. Therefore, it may make sense to speak of God as dog or God as plant, but it would be pointless for _us_ to talk about God in these terms. So, for us, the most sensible thing to do, if we choose to talk about God at all, is to talk about God as person.

What is involved when we speak of God as person? At first the distinction between God as person and God being a person was not made. In Greek mythology the gods were conceived as being super persons. At present, as far as sophisticated religious thinkers are concerned, to think of God as person is to make the following claim, no matter how tenuous this claim may be: God, to be God, must be open to the full range of human experience. For theism it would make no sense to assert that God would find certain human experiences incomprehensible. We find humans incomprehensible and unintelligible in varying degrees but then we are not God, and any creatures with these limitations could not be God. A major part of what the mature religious believer believes--and this is essential for his devotional and prayer life--is that no matter what he feels, no matter what he hopes for, no matter what he fears, God will understand and sympathize with him, which is _not_ the same as saying that God will necessarily approve of the feeling or the action. To have a concept of God as person is to entertain a concept of divinity which sees God as fully _aware_ of the full range of human experience. Nothing that happens to humans could fail to be understood and apprehended by God.

Another aspect of this matter can be approached through a further use of analogy along lines developed by Hartshorne. Let us use for this analogy the example of a dog again, only this time the relation of the dog to his human master. In the best circumstances there is a relation of mutual affection between the two. Both the dog and his owner are finite creatures, of course, so there are limits to their apprehension of each other. While there are aspects of doglike experience which are closed to humans there are vastly more aspects of human experience which as far as we can tell are closed to dogs. The relationship between the dog and his owner must be carried out on the dog's terms through such things as feeding and petting the dog, training it to do tricks or to guard the children. While the dog may be present in the room it is presumably incapable of being aware that its owner is proving mathematical theorems, enjoying Bartok string quartets or making out his income tax. These experiences, though carried out in the presence of the dog, transcend the ability of the dog to apprehend. Yet during the processes of these human experiences which are basically closed to the dog, the master may pet the dog, feed it and involve himself in a relationship with the dog at the level at which the dog can relate to and apprehend him. The human master is both imminent and transcendent as far as the dog's experience is concerned. The dog may relate with much affection to his master, but most of what his master is, is forever closed to the dog.

It is not difficult to see the analogy here between man and God. The relationship between man and God must be basically at our level because of our limitations, for this is the only thing which could make sense to us. To the extent to which man and God are in mutual relationship to each other, God is imminent in our experience and because we are persons this relationship involves us with God as person. But as orthodoxy has pointed out, if God is person, he is much more besides. God as transcendent has features of which we can never be aware--they are closed to us presumably in some way analogous to which much of our experience is closed to a dog. Just as a dog could apprehend what it is to be a human only to a very limited extent, we can apprehend God only to an extremely limited extent.

The analogy we have used cannot be pressed too far and must not be misunderstood. Some alert reader might say that since we apprehend God as person, if the analogy holds we would be forced into the absurdity of saying that a dog apprehends his master as dog, and this seems to be very odd, and yet there is a sense in which I want to maintain that this is true in both cases no matter how odd it may sound at first. We said earlier that man apprehends God as person, but that this is quite different from saying that God is a person. Part of what we meant was that man can apprehend God only in the highest terms which relate to himself. In a somewhat similar way I would maintain that a dog apprehends his master _as_ dog, which is not the same as to say that he apprehends his master as _a_ dog, which he most obviously does not. What is meant is that a dog apprehends his master in the only way in which a dog can, that he meets his master in the context of receiving food, petting on the head, training to jump over obstacles, but never as the creator of a work of art. A dog apprehends man as only a dog can. Also while man is not a dog, man like dog knows what it is to be hungry, to jump over obstacles, to have fear and to receive pleasure. To the extent that a man can share experiences similar to those of a dog, to that extent, man can be apprehended as dog. In the same way to the extent that God can share similar experiences to a man, God can rightfully be apprehended as person.

There are, of course, points of disanalogy, for the analogy was only made to bring out certain features of personalistic theism. While to some extent we can share similar basic experiences with a dog, and can enter into satisfactory relationships with dogs, we are, to a large extent, as ignorant of what it is to be a dog as the dog is ignorant of what it is to be a man; still it would seem that we have a better idea of what it is to be a dog than a dog could have of what it is to be a man. If theists are right the analogy breaks down at this point. While we would be in great ignorance about what it is to be God, God would have a peculiarly intimate insight into what it would be like to be a person. It is important to keep the limits of the analogy in mind, for God's knowledge of creatures would be radically distinct from the knowledge that any finite creature has of another whether this be of man to man or of man to dog. While the relationship between a man and a dog must be carried out in terms which can "make sense" to the dog, and while a man far surpasses a dog, still there is a great deal about dogs which is intrinsically mystifying to men. While the relations between man and God must be carried out in a manner that man can grasp, it would seem unlikely that there is much, if anything, that is intrinsically mystifying about man, as far as God is concerned. This is an important point of disanalogy to keep in mind. God's knowledge is categorically distinct from the knowledge that any finite creature has of any other creature, but from this it does not follow that we cannot draw some kinds of analogies between human and divine knowledge.

Most theists would argue that nothing is closed to God and that our most intimate experiences are open to him. While this is a speculative matter I would want to argue that while this is true to a major extent, each person may have to have a modicum of privacy in his own experience, even from God. The reason I say this is the fear that if you make everything directly open to God in most intimate privacy, pluralistic personalism may collapse into a religious monism. This is a major philosophic issue in itself, but it may be the case that part of being a person is to have some area of privacy not only in relation to others, but in relation to God as well. I would suggest that metaphysically part of being a person is to have some experiences private to oneself--that there must be some degree of hiddenness to others. This obviously seems to be the case when we are speaking of the relation of one person to another; where it becomes problematical is in relations of persons to God. That God would have much that is private to him and not open to persons is a point that scarcely needs laboring, but what we must deal with is the question as to whether persons are "open to God' in an absolute sense or not. Orthodoxy would maintain that complete openness to God is essential if one is to maintain divine omnipotence. This does not seem an essential point to hold if one embraces some variant of dipolar theism.

It is quite obvious that a question like this is purely speculative. All that we can do is to develop what seems to be a consistent and coherent view of the nature of God and of his relation to the world. If the intimate privacy of my own experience is completely open to God in an absolute sense--that is to say if God experiences my experiences with literally the same immediacy that I do, then a number of consequences might ensue, some of which seem implausible in the light of experience. One consequence which many have accepted would be a monistic pantheism. The absence of privacy would seem to involve a merging of every consciousness into the one over-all divine consciousness. While monistic pantheism has been a philosophical and religious position of long standing, it would seem to conflict radically with an empiricism which points towards an obvious pluralism. The other important aspect concerning the privacy of our own experience is the essential pluralism involved in the I-Thou encounter of man and God. Devotional and prayer life is in the profoundest sense a life of dialogue and it takes two to dialogue. One might still object that this does not entail the privacy of man to God. It is often said that God knows what man will ask before he asks it--and there is a sense surely in which God sees into the innermost heart of man. To admit this, however, is not to admit necessarily that the experiences of God and man are identical in all their intimacy and privacy. In the quite literal sense if God knew all that was in a man's heart there would be no point in a human-divine dialogue. It would seem to be a doing over again what had already been done, at least from God's perspective. A main factor of dialogue and prayer is <u>disclosure</u>, not only of oneself to oneself, but to the other as well. For this there must be something private--something to disclose.

Take the analogy of a parent and child. A parent can have a very good idea of what a child wants or feels before the child articulates it and yet in the sheer act of articulation a new relationship between self and self is set up, involving added disclosure of what is private. We must beware of pushing the analogy too far, but it is useful as far as it goes. God knows man immeasurably better than a parent can know his child, but I would still want to maintain that the knowledge is not absolute, even here. While God's knowledge of creatures immeasurably exceeds that of all other creatures in a categorically distinct way, one may still doubt that it encompasses the privacy of the other, for to do this would be to destroy the essential personhood of the other and the duality found in the I-Thou relationship. It would seem as though the "I-Thou" encounter, whether it be between man and man or between man and God involves an essential element of surprise as well as an essential pluralism meaning privacy. In this kind of dyadic relationship it really takes two centers of personality to relate to each other in the modes of prayer, meditation and communion.

Admittedly this seems "far out" and most thinkers, whether of a monopolar or dipolar persuasion would contend that nothing can be hidden from God or not be known to God. Nevertheless, I simply want to suggest the possiblity that personhood may mean privacy in some respects from the other, even if the other is God. I see nothing self-contradictory about such an idea unless one builds into the concept of God to begin with that he is all seeing and all knowing. And from a Whiteheadean perspective, even if God knows all that has occurred in the past and what is occurring at present, God, too, must wait for the future to unfold before grasping it with full knowledge. Whether one accepts this point about privacy or not, it is still the case that in the I-Thou encounter between man and God, the dialogue may be most important for man to have. Man needs to unburden himself before God, whether God is all knowing or not.

A crucial character of God as Person is utter <u>dependability</u>. Most human beings have a relatively stable character and personality on which we can rely. The degree of reliability varies widely from person to person and of course the character qualities on which we rely in other persons run from those of which we approve to those of which we do not. A person may be predictably kind, generous and outgoing or predictably stingy, angry and sadistic. In either case, we develop certain expectations about others and these expectations are borne out in varying degrees, but in each person the unexpected and out-of-character pops up from time to time too. While not synonymous, dependability and predictability generally go together, as far as humans are concerned. We can depend on another person, to the degree that we can successfully predict what he is likely to do in given situations. Conversely, to the extent that we are unable to predict behavior, the person is undependable in this regard. While the variations between persons are very great, no human being is absolutely predictable or dependable. A basic part of the human condition is that we fail to be absolutely dependable to others, no matter how hard we try--hence guilt and human finitude. Dependability also means something more than simply reliability and predictability. If this were all it meant a table would be more dependable than a person. Part of what is meant is that one can count on another person for aid, sympathy and understanding, and that the other will not turn away from you in disgust, anger or out of boredom, denying your essential personhood. As humans, no one is dependable in an absolute sense and all of us fail others at some time or other.

God as person is the paradigm case of utter or absolute dependability--this is an essential quality in any kind of personalistic theism. The most obvious objection to this comes from what we saw early in this study.[1] God's grace is radically unpredictable (Minimal Thirdness) and if we have been equating predictability and dependability it would seem to follow that God, for many, is radically undependable as well. Yet if this is held to without qualification, a main aspect of personalistic theism seems to go by the board. As we have seen, in the religious experience of many persons God's manifestation is often radically unpredictable. While unpredictability and undependability generally go together, they are not identical in meaning.

For many believers God is frequently absent; indeed, for many mystics he has often been inexplicably absent. One has only to read the Book of Job or the mystical literature on the "dark night of the soul" to realize this. For many such persons, however, God's dependability does <u>not</u> mean that God will <u>predictably</u> appear or manifest himself in a way that the believer expects and desires. Here God's dependability means that for a believer, the divine absence never denotes lack of interest in or boredom with the believer or inability on the part of God to relate to the believer. It means Job's affirmation, "Though he slay me, yet will I trust him." It is true that God may be displeased with the believer, but even this does not mean that God is unreliable in the way that people turn out to be. If one meant by dependable that God must act in the particular way that a given individual would desire, then God, too, would be undependable. When we think carefully about this we realize that it would be childish to expect God to respond as we wish. What the religious believer has faith in is that no matter how unpredictable God may be, he has not turned his face away from man in boredom or disgust. Utter dependability means that the believer will continue to have faith in God no matter how peculiar things look empirically. The believer will have faith that God as person will be utterly dependable in the sense that he is always concerned and related to man, no matter how unpredictable God is.

This is precisely what makes faith and the problem of evil so excruciating. It is precisely the existence of negative evidence (evil) which makes the issue insoluble as far as classical theism is concerned and soluble but still excruciating as far as dipolar theism is concerned. If God is thought of as undependable then theism might as well give up the ghost and yet it is precisely this quality in God which demands the most in terms of faith on the part of the believer. For many, dependability is a real property of God, no matter how hidden. Thus, as we have seen, though God is unpredictable, it does not follow that for the believer he is undependable. Phenomenologically this would seem to be the case as far as many religious persons are concerned. "God's ways are not our ways" refers to his otherness and unpredictability. God's dependability is a function of one's faith or lack of it.

To sum up this discussion of God as person, we can say that God can encompass and understand the whole range of human personhood and emotional response. To say that God is not to be seen as person in any sense is to leave open the possibility that humans may surpass God in crucial respects. If the universe is impersonal, then man, even though he may be crushed by that universe, is superior to it, as Pascal pointed out, for man is a "thinking reed," and the universe is not. To this degree anthropomorphism is essential to a doctrine of God. To settle for less is to abandon the point of theism; to push on towards a gross anthropomorphism is again to make God just like man and, thus, allow man to surpass God, as happened with the gods of Mt Olympus. In short, God must be seen as person, but this is not to say that he is a person. Perhaps one could say that God as immanent is seen as person, but God as transcendent is not.

NOTES

1 See Chapter 4.

CHAPTER 8

THE PROBLEM OF EVIL REVISITED

> Look round this universe. What an immense profusion of beings, animated and organized, sensible and active! You admire this prodigious variety and fecundity. But inspect a little more narrowly these living existences, the only beings worth regarding. How hostile and destructive to each other! How insufficient all of them for their own happiness! How contemptible or odious to the spectator! The whole presents nothing but the idea of a blind nature, impregnated by a great vivifying principle, and pouring forth from her lap, without discernment or parental care, her maimed and abortive children![1]

In this passage and others like it in his "Dialogues," Hume, through the mouths of Demea and Philo, dramatically sketches the grim picture of massive evils, natural and man-made, which experience presents to us, casting doubt on the optimism of the eighteenth century as well as on the argument from design defended in the "Dialogues" by Cleanthes. If the picture as presented in the eighteenth century was grim, it is even more so in our own time. The theological and philosophical problem of evil has been wrestled with over the ages resulting in various solutions and criticism of proposed solutions. We need to revisit this problem because its nagging urgency is not only a major threat to faith commitment but the existence of evil threatens the development of any consistent religious viewpoint that seeks some philosophical defense.

We can briefly recap why there is felt to be a philosophical or theological problem of evil. The problem is most severe in the context of theism which embraces a personal God and most notable in traditional classical theism. If God is analogous to a father or person and is all-powerful and all good, how is it possible that natural and man-made evils exist at all? That such evils do exist is patently obvious. If God is all-powerful why doesn't he prevent evil? If he is also all good why doesn't he prevent it? One could soften the severity of the problem by giving up either God's supreme power or his supreme goodness. To give up the divine goodness, even in part, would be to destroy theism. To give up the supreme power would destroy an axiom of classical theism. However, dipolar theism goes a long way towards resolving the problem by developing a concept of God limited in power, hence less responsible for evil. As we shall see later, the problem remains unresolved with dipolar theism, but this view is far preferable to the classical view.

Where no personal theistic God is involved, the philosophical problem of evil is radically reduced in severity but not eliminated. I am thinking here of pantheistic views that are characteristic of Hinduism and Buddhism and certain types of nature mysticism. In such views there is a spiritual force or forces that one can "tap into" through meditation and self-discipline, but these forces are not necessarily personal nor are they guaranteed to accord respect and concern to individual persons. Furthermore, in various kinds of pantheism, individual personality is regarded as an illusion to be overcome by achieving a sense of unity with the whole. Reincarnation doctrines in pantheism also allow for an unending amount of time to achieve enlightenment. Still, no individual personhood is preserved and though the universe is thought to be spiritual and good, the immensity of suffering and evil mocks the pantheistic pretension that the universe is basically good and spiritual in character.

If one turns to any kind of philosophical naturalism, the philosophical and theological problem of evil evaporates, in fact it does not arise at all. There is a severe practical problem to be sure; this is so in all views, but naturalism has no philosophical or theological problem to face. Since, in this view, the universe is neither good nor bad as a whole but value neutral, the only problem is how to cope with evil. Thus, for our purposes we can leave naturalism aside.

When one returns to religious views the philosophical problem of explaining evil arises in its various forms. Most attempted resolutions remain implausible because the amount and nature of human suffering in the world is prima facie at variance with the view that the world as a whole is spiritual and good. Attempts to explain evil away as unreal and illusion are farcical in the light of experience. Nor does the view that separate selfhood is the source of evil and suffering provide a solution. It is true that egocentricity and selfishness produce much pointless suffering, but selfhood per se is what allows for creativity and development and for the joys of entering into community with others. Empirically, theism is more plausible about the self than holistic pantheism because genuine selfhood and individuality are preserved in a pluralistic world. Of the various religious options, dipolar theism seems the most coherent outlook to adopt in dealing with evil. Roughly, if God is limited in power in some respects, he is less responsible for evil than if he has infinite power in all respects.

But even dipolar theism underrates the significance and importance of evil for any kind of religious viewpoint. There remains a basic incoherence between what religious views of the world maintain and the obvious facts of evil that exist massively in our world. For very good reasons, many lose faith when confronted with the enormity of the situation. A friend of mine who had been in the Polish resistance against the Nazis in World War II put it very succinctly: the existence of the world we live in is a condemnation of religion--there could not be a God and have such a world as we do. While concentrating on the extent and nature of evil, we must not forget that there is a vast amount of good in the world--that human happiness and community do exist but these are features that one would expect in a divinely ordered world, and, thus, do not cry out for explanation.

The sheer quantitative amount of human suffering and pain is overwhelming. The evidence of this is obvious for all to see. In addition to the individual hells that we concoct for ourselves and our families, the social evils of society dwarf all others. War, racism and human exploitation have been with us for centuries and their abatement is not a marked feature of contemporary life. Natural evils such as those produced by accident, lingering illness and ultimately death have been and are a permanent part of the human condition. Deliberate man-made evils are even more pervasive producing thousands of innocent victims. One need only mention the sufferings brought on by world-wide drug abuse, warfare, human exploitation and the great disparities of wealth between the haves and the have nots. The quality of human life, indeed, human life itself, is in jeopardy. If the bomb does not get us in the end, the probability of polluting our environment beyond repair is a real possibility. Think for a moment of the degree to which the economies of the world depend on war and armaments and on the production of illegal drugs, not to mention legal drugs that are dispensed to make life bearable for many. In the technologically advanced countries of the world, the dehumanizing aspects of mass culture are ever more apparent while in many underdeveloped third world countries, tribal roots and loyalties are destroyed and opportunistic dictators proliferate to take advantage of desperate populations.

True, in technologically advanced countries the standard of living of the ordinary person dwarfs the wildest dreams of his ancestors but at a social cost in loss of spiritual roots and of family and community support which is staggering. In our own culture, belief in freedom and liberty translates itself into gross and mindless self-indulgence encouraged and abetted by advertising, huckstering and salesmanship. Our standard for public service seems to be to find a person who has not actually been convicted of outright fraud or theft. We are told to consume and be happy but a licit and illicit drug trade gives testimony to our unhappiness and desperation. The quality of life is degraded by overcrowding and by pollution. The assumption of common moral standards and the habits of civility towards others are rapidly eroding. Note the increased tendency towards litigation for all kinds of reasons, often trivial, and the increasing number of situations in which people see themselves in adversarial relationships towards others, maintaining that they have extensive entitlement rights towards almost everything. We increasingly use up the world's resources with little or no concern for the social or environmental costs involved. As advanced technological cultures in the west begin to develop the first glimmers of sensitivity towards environmental issues, the third world feels, with considerable justification, that it is time to "get their innings" as far as development and exploitation of natural resources are concerned. Having plundered the world for two centuries, western technological culture is looked at as being hypocritical in its growing environmental concern. The third world accuses us of shedding crocodile tears about the environment--having amassed our wealth already while the third world has yet to do so. In general, communist states have not done better and such societies have proved disastrous where instituted. They can only be maintained by a continuation of force and overwhelming social conditioning. If animals and plants could articulate their experiences of the world they might well see humans as cancerous cells spreading over the earth and destroying everything in their path.

We do not like to accept the picture I have presented for it presents us as the enemy of all that exists and implicates us radically in evil and yet nothing I have pointed out is unknown to any reasonably well-informed person. Viewed empirically and dispassionately, humans seem to be a species on the road to self-destruction. Surely this is a one-sided view. Yes, it is. There are many redeeming features in humans individually and collectively. Great civilizations have produced art, religion, science and technology. We have produced much of value but it is an open question as to whether the forces for betterment are powerful enough to overcome the destructive forces I have mentioned. The human race does not seem to be much better or worse than it ever was. Perhaps we would have destroyed ourselves long ago if we had had the technological knowledge and ability to do so. Now we do have that knowledge. Man is neither saint nor devil but an odd mixture. Man may not be sunk in sin as Calvinists believed, but he is certainly neither inherently rational nor good, as Socrates believed.

After this grim catalogue of human evil it may pay us to remind ourselves again of the good features of humanity just to keep a sense of perspective. Close human personal relations at their best make everything we have to live through worthwhile. There are many families and other kinds of small community where fellowship, common concerns and love abide in large degree. The whole area of the richness of experience needs to be mentioned. By this I mean what was called the aesthetic dimension in the eighteenth century which includes a lot more than artistic creativity and enjoyment. There is richness and variety in human experiences of enjoyment and satisfaction individually and in groups. Last but not least there is the satisfaction found in striving for excellence and mastery, overcoming obstacles expressed in the creative urges of man. These positive human goods are not to be ignored or short changed, even when brought to an end by illness and death, for while they last these values have an intrinsic goodness about them. If an omnipotent devil ruled the world you would have a demonological problem of explaining these goods just as with an omnipotent God you have a problem of explaining evil.

All such goods are transitory and subject to destruction and this fact drives humans towards the religious dimension. Another urgent factor that drives them towards this dimension is the basic unfairness of life--that the goods and evils of the world fall on the just and the unjust by no rhyme or reason or merit or worth of the persons involved. Whether one agrees with him or not, one can appreciate Unamuno's passionate feeling that religion is about personal immortality or it is worth nothing.[2] Many feel strongly that the basic unfairness of life must be resolved religiously by some kind of doctrine of reincarnation or immortality so that eventually all get what they deserve. Who can say whether such restitution occurs? What is apparent is that one of the greatest evils of life is its unfairness and injustice. From a naturalistic perspective one can only respond that this is just the way things are. But if the world manifests divinity surely some kind of restitution on the basis of justice and equity can be hoped for and be believed in. To take natural and man-made evil seriously and to realize its extent and dimensions presents a real anguish for anyone, be he pantheist or theist, who regards the world as governed by a beneficent force or forces.

Let us break the problem of evil down into two components for purposes of clarification. The two components are natural evils and man-made evils. Examples of natural evils would be lingering illness and death, earthquakes, floods and fires, all kinds of natural disasters and accidents which happen to persons but which are not brought about by the deliberate intentions of persons, nor as an unintended by-product of human acts of dominance and self-assertion. Natural evils seem to be a logical part of a pluralistic world with different kinds of creatures with various and conflicting values. If you are going to have anything that could recognizably be called a world, it will contain conflicting values, only some of which can be actualized, often at the expense of other values. Leibniz explained this conflict in terms of compossibility. Not everything that is logically possible in the abstract is possible together in the concrete. You don't have to have a world with water in it or human beings in it, but you can't have both water and humans without the possibility that humans may drown in the water, as well as be nourished and cleansed by it. You don't have to have animals in a world, but if you do, then they must eat something. You don't have to have a world with humans in it, but if you do, they will embody conflicting interests and centers of value realization which cannot all be actualized. You cannot have meaningful choice of any kind without erasing the alternative possibilities which went unchosen. A child wants everything at once and finds it hard to see why good things cannot be easily obtained and bad things avoided. As adults we know better. The tragedy of life is that you cannot actualize everything because things that are chosen can only be chosen at the expense of many other often good things that must remain unchosen.

Compossibility was one reason Leibniz argued that this is the best of all possible worlds for which he was mercilessly satirized. The other reason Leibniz had to argue that this is the best of all possible worlds was that his commitment to classical theism demanded it. If God is all-powerful and all good then he would be radically implicated in evil if he failed to make the best possible world an actuality. Obviously the world could be better than it is or there would be no point in doing anything. One cannot make any sense out of human action if one does not assume that the actor expects by his actions to make the world somewhat better than it is already. This holds even if he is, in fact, mistaken and ends up making the world worse. Though Leibniz is mistaken about the best of all possible worlds, his insight into compossibility is a profound one. The concept of a perfect world is a contradiction in terms, like a round square. Anything we could understand to be a world at all which contained any animals or persons would by its nature be imperfect--that is, it would contain felt evil and loss for its creatures as well as gain and joy. A perfect world could at best be a static Platonic Form, for any change could only be for the worse. The whole notion of action and doing would lose its point. Even the God of classical theism, as perfect, must remain static, changeless and eternal--a religious absurdity as Charles Hartshorne has pointed out again and again. How _much_ natural evil there has to be in a world remains a mystery. But since compossibility limits how good the world can become it makes no sense to insist that God remove all natural evil from the world.

Now let us turn to the issue of man-made evils, ones that are either the result of deliberate action by humans, or evil produced as an unintended side effect of deliberate human action or inaction (the failure to do something that needed to be done but was not done). Man-made evils seem to have a perversity about them that engenders moral outrage, for these are felt in many cases to be avoidable--not that some natural evils cannot be avoided too, but the avoidance of man-made evil seems particularly urgent and calls out for relief against injustices perpetrated. For example, airplane accidents will occur even with the best planning because of wind sheer or the plane being struck by lightning, but if the accident is due to negligence or dishonesty our moral outrage legitimately boils forth. Illness can be reduced and flood control plans put in place, but with all precautions taken, natural evils and fluke accidents will continue to occur. They are tragic in their results, but they do not engender the moral outrage produced by the tragic results of corruption, dishonesty and greed. We feel these man-made evils should not be allowed to occur and when they do occur it is felt that justice should be rendered. Man-made evils are directly produced by us and we are responsible for them. This is so even while we recognize that any particular generation inherits and is conditioned by the social arrangements given to it. We can understand why our ancestors accepted slavery, but this does not mean that we should accept it now or that they should have then.

Man-made evils, particularly large scale social evils, compound the theological and philosophical difficulties when added to those of natural evils. Indeed, the immensities of human suffering are difficult to square with any concept of divinity unless one takes a purely Manichaeian view of the situation. Granted that compossibility entails some suffering and pain, one still is left wondering why the amount of it has to be so extensive. Could not a loving father God have produced a world with considerably less risk and pain than the one we live in? Must the margins for human safety and survival be so narrowly drawn? This is a crucial point that Hume raises in his "Dialogues." Even slight changes in climate and weather could doom the human race. As we have seen, while there is spiritual growth through suffering--indeed, one might argue that suffering is essential to spiritual growth--does this justify the intensity and amount of human suffering that exists? Probably many more are destroyed by suffering than achieve growth through it. Even reincarnation doctrines do not justify evil or set one's mind more at ease, for reincarnation may simply mean an endless continuation of human miseries in different form. And when one returns to the Christian tradition, the sacredness of human persons as children of God certainly does not square with the dimensions of human anguish.

Does the human condition per se entail such costs? Human anguish may be the cost of having humans in the world at all. Augustine saw this point when he contended that it is better to have man sinning than not to have man at all. Are persons by their nature so constructed that they cannot avoid building civilizations that are so destructive of human values? Being human seems to involve a basic perversity towards others in terms of ego gratification and the desire for power and control. It looks as though human achievement particularly in competitive areas can only be bought at the expense of less human achievement by others. If our society is to prevail it is only through making other societies weaker so that they will not prevail. Since they too want to prevail, we have a clash of wills, which more often than not is settled by overwhelming force or by stalemate if the powers brought to bear are more or less equal. Indeed, both Hobbes and Sartre argue that human selfishness and assertiveness are so bad that human community can only arise through fear and dire necessity. Both thinkers argue that it is only the threat of anarchy and the "other" that brings humans into community at all, and then only as long as the threat remains. Coupled with massive amounts of Sartrean bad faith, modern nation states and communities seem to follow the Sartrean model.

Humans seem to do much better when taken as individuals than as groups. Sartre's view of the individual's desire to dominate others is clearly overstated. Most of us as individuals enter into spontaneous community with others in terms of mutual friendship and consideration. The loving and open family is the model of human community at its best even though many families are anything but open and loving. Community organizations of various kinds based on a mutuality of interest and not based on antagonism towards others thrive throughout the world but it is the larger more paranoid communities such as nation states, corporations, the Mafia, fanatical religious states and political parties which seem to dominate the scene and account in large part for the miseries forced upon mankind.

Given a religious orientation towards the world a number of remaining observations are in order. If action and choice are real, then it would seem that real risks have to be recognized as coming out of those choices. Part of real choice seems to be the ability to "go for broke" individually as well as in terms of our collective decision making. Trivial choices involve trivial consequences if failure occurs. Great and far-reaching choices involve hair-raising consequences if failure occurs. To build a modern society along technological lines may give us undreamed of freedom and creative possibilities, but the risks of failure and disaster are obvious. Danger and opportunity go hand in hand and compossibility seems to allow us no escape from this. Still, we want to ask, couldn't God have set limits to the destructive capabilities of mankind, the way a loving parent sets limits to the amount of damage a small child is allowed to risk? Classical theism has no out here, for a loving parent is finite and even setting limits cannot avoid possible disaster for the child. An omnipotent God in all respects remains unavoidably implicated in evil. Compossibility on the other hand may set intrinsic limits to the reduction of man-made evils. Classical theism is caught in the bind that nothing can be allowed to set limits on God. Once this "hangup" is removed, we can speak coherently of compossibility and the dipolar God.

Even accepting the insights behind compossibility combined with a dipolar view of the nature of God, we have good reason to think that the maximization of value is far from reached. If such maximization had been reached, only change for the worse could occur. Granted all of this, there still seems to be an incredible distance between where we are at present and a maximum of compossible goods. Nothing of value is achievable without risks, but even so the risks in the world are appalling, and the evils involved cannot allow for an easy or complacent acceptance.

Perhaps we should speak of the compossibility factor in more concrete terms. One could not have nuclear power and nuclear medicine without also having the capability of making nuclear bombs. The large-scale social institutions which produce widespread social evils are also able to produce much good, which they could not produce if they were not large scale. Indeed modern technology itself is large scale. Modern technology has raised the standard of material living to unbelievable degrees and if what we are told is so, could wipe world hunger from the face of the earth. Technology is already being used to reduce pollution in the environment that earlier it itself produced, but as these benefits are provided, advancing technology continues to produce pollution and various other anti-social side effects. The goods of technology have to be purchased by the bad side effects of technology and it is a real question as to whether the bad side effects will outweigh the good in the future. The Club of Rome and other experts have made dire predictions about what will happen with unlimited economic and technological growth. Another dire result of advancing technology is the so-called "greenhouse effect" where pollutants lead to the increased heating of the earth with the resultant rise in ocean levels as the polar ice caps melt. As we have already indicated, though technology has produced and can continue to produce the highest material standard of living in the world, it is far from obvious that it increases the quality of such living--indeed, it may have reduced it drastically. However, to increase the material standard of living from semi-starvation is no mean feat. To eliminate hunger and starvation alone would vastly increase the quality of life. But beyond a certain level, technology alone will not improve the quality of life, but may destroy it. It is not technology alone that produces many of the bad side effects, but the social policies and spiritual aridity that go along with it. A high material standard of living can and often does free human beings for creative and exciting lives that they would otherwise not have if they had to live from hand to mouth, but more frequently it releases human beings into a world of boredom where self-indulgent cheap thrills are sought to make life bearable.

There is no necessary reason why technology itself must produce vapid and immature entertainment, immoral huckstering and cultural uniformity at a very mediocre level. There is no necessary reason why technology has to be used to turn out better weapons of mass destruction. There is no necessary reason why technology has to turn out products that are unsafe and poorly constructed. There is no necessary reason why technology has to produce space capsules that explode on take off due to careless construction.

There are other features of technology however where compossibility limitations do enter. It is hard to see how industrial development and living standards in Africa and South America can be significantly raised without attendant destruction of the tropical rain forests and dire consequences that arise from that. It is hard to see how growing energy needs can be met at present without the development of dangerous nuclear power plants or the pollution attendant on the development of more fossil fuels. Possibly a serious development of solar energy in the future might get around this. It is hard to see how technological development can increase without increasing the "greenhouse effect." It is hard to see how we can continue to have a disposable "throw away" culture without increasing our pollution problems to dangerous degrees. Likewise it is hard to see how we can afford to continue use of chemical pesticides and fertilizers without dire consequences to the environment. It is hard to see how we can grow increasingly reliant on drugs, legal and illegal, without destroying human personality and community. It is hard to see how we can continue our love affair with the automobile without making the environment more and more undesirable as a place to live.

As human beings we have hard choices to make, trade-offs of one good against other goods. No matter what is done, real sacrifice of some values is unavoidable as is tragedy and human loss. Such is the iron logic of compossibility. But nothing about compossibility entails that things have to be as staggeringly bad as in fact they are.

All of this presents real difficulty for all of us, but special difficulties for those <u>who see the world in religious terms</u>. Though one might like to argue otherwise, neither naturalism nor religion has an intrinsically preferred status provable from the nature of things. Both represent human perspectives on the world that arise out of human experience and as we have indicated before, experience is fraught with ambiguity and gives no clear message. This is precisely why for religious persons evil presents such severe philosophical and theological perplexity.

As for ambiguity, why not take the existence of evils as intimations of the demonic or at least as intimations of cosmic absurdity? This, of course, is frequently done and one has only to think of such astute thinkers as Sartre, Camus and the Bertrand Russell of "A Free Man's Worship." Frankly there is as much justification for reading experience this way as for reading experience religiously. But James has said that no philosophy can gain general assent which forever frustrates our deepest hopes and wishes. Can we be as sure of this as James was? His outlook may have had more plausibility in 1900 than it does now. After what the human race has been through in the last fifty years and the bleak prospects for it in the future, many would feel that <u>intimations of absurdity</u> would be more appropriate to speak about than <u>intimations of divinity</u>. When one adds to this the pervasive fact of death at the end of the road for all of us no matter how we are situated, the case for absurdity begins to assume compelling proportions. There is no need here to re-document the staggering amount of evil and tragedy that occurs both at the individual and at the collective level. Yet, as Alan Watts has pointed out, human suffering is distributive, not composite. We speak of suffering humanity and in a sense millions do suffer and yet in another sense <u>only individuals</u> suffer. This does not mitigate the immensities of suffering and tragedy, but I think it is worth pointing out in the interests of perspective.

Naturalism makes perfectly good sense. It is a persuasive view of the world and the bulk of experience would seem to point to a value ambiguous world. For a person committed to empiricism and rational intelligent appraisal, naturalism makes the most sense, particularly if one wants to use an Occum's razor principle and make minimal ontological commitments as to the value status of the universe. Those who stress <u>absurdity</u> seem to be disappointed and angry because their expectations of the universe went unfulfilled. Nietzsche and Sartre both responded as though God or the universe had violated a contract that was to assure them that the universe was ultimately not absurd. Nietzsche is angry and Sartre accepts his "dreadful freedom." Who but a disappointed theist could say that "if God is dead all is permitted"? You can make a strong argument that anyone who stresses the absurdity of existence has expected too much from the world to begin with. Why demand that we come into the world with some guarantee against tragedy? This attitude trivializes tragedy and evil just as much as does a fatuous religious optimism. Positivism may be more profound at this point. Why even regard the world as absurd? It may be simply value ambiguous and one had better do the best one can with the empirical realities that one confronts.

In the "Dialogues Concerning Natural Religion," Hume indicates that there are four possible options one might take regarding the value status of the universe. One could regard it as value positive--governed by a divine principle, value negative--governed by a supreme demonic principle, both value positive and value negative--Manichaeianism or neither value positive nor value negative--naturalism. In Hume's view the ambivalent nature of experience rules out the value positive and value negative positions and interestingly enough Manichaeianism is ruled out because of the orderly lawlike nature of the universe, thus leaving only the naturalistic option open. As I have already indicated a tough minded empiricist with a propensity for Occum's razor will embrace naturalism. Intimations of God or devil will be rejected and a demand for hard evidence will be made. Intimations of absurdity are just as tenuous as intimations of divinity.

I would prefer to speak of the universe as value ambivalent. What needs stressing at this point is the "far out" character of theistic faith. Because religious belief has been so pervasive we have come to take it for granted. The religious perspective in general and the Christian perspective in particular are extreme and deviant ones in crucial ways as Kierkegaard never tired of indicating. Particularly in the light of tragedy and suffering it is extremely odd, to put it mildly, to have faith in a divine being whose pervasive love and concern is ubiquitous. What is really astounding is that people should have intimations of divinity at all, let alone religious faith--but they do. Do suffering and evil count against the theistic perspective? Certainly. This is one reason a purely a priori theology will not do. This is why there is a place for an empirical theology. This is precisely what makes the leap of faith so risky. Only a fool could make such a leap if it were not for the intimations of divinity. Are there intimations that would count against divinity? Certainly. There are intimations of absurdity as well. But even if one opts in a religious direction, a mature theism will never underestimate the evil and tragedy which are real and which, prima facie, point away from a theistic orientation. Intimations of absurdity are the reverse side of the coin of intimations of divinity. Only one who had expected and hoped for divinity and been disappointed could call the world absurd. The thinkers of absurdity show prime evidence of major religious frustration. There are aspects of experience that point in both directions, and each aspect in a kind of Hegelian way demands the other. The search for divinity is pursued by those who are struggling to overcome the felt absurdity of things. The acceptance of absurdity occurs in those who have yearned for the divine and felt no intimations of divinity. Positivistic naturalism has felt the pull of neither side--for it the world is neither divine nor absurd. The Russell of "A Free Man's Worship" felt the tug of the absurd, the later Russell in his philosophical writings did not, though this element continues to be present in his popular political writings. That the sense of the divine and of the absurd are two sides of a coin can be seen also in those who feel the tug of both intimations. That is why in the broad sense we can say that Sartre, Nietzsche and Kierkegaard are all religious thinkers. Possibly the only kinds of non-religious perspectives in this broad sense are the various schools of positivism and empirical naturalism.

What must be fully faced and accepted is that the religious choice of faith does fly in the face of massive evils, both natural and man-made. In the face of such evils, many do, quite sensibly, lose their faith. For them, evil seems to disconfirm any religious view of the world whatsoever, but this is not disconfirmation in any rigorous scientific sense of the term. Others, like Job, in the face of evil do not drop their faith, and they are not being irrational in the sense that a fundamentalist who rejects evolution is being irrational. To make a religious faith commitment is not, per se, to reject the findings of science. While precise disconfirmation is not involved, evil does present severe existential and emotional difficulties for the religious believer. Interestingly enough, evil may not only drive many away from religion, it may also drive others towards the religious in the way in which the founder of Quakerism, George Fox, saw "an ocean of darkness and death covered over by an ocean of light." For the religious person evil remains a burning issue, existentially always threatening faith, but this does not make evil a philosophical or theological problem, if you mean by "problem" something that even theoretically has a solution. Even dipolar theism is not a solution to the problem of evil, though dipolar theism can reduce some of the tension of incoherence in theological doctrine. Evil is not a problem to be solved; it is something that has to be lived through with agony and resolution.

NOTES

[1] David Hume, "Dialogues Concerning Natural Religion" in _The English Philosophers from Bacon to Mill_, ed. E. A. Burtt (New York: Random House, 1939) p. 751.

[2] See Miguel De Unamuno, _The Tragic Sense of Life_ (New York: Dover Publications, 1954).

CHAPTER 9

DIVINITY AS A GIVEN

Heidegger maintains that ours is a time in which the "gods have fled." Among other things he means to refer to the dominant secularism of our modern technological society. A strong sense of divine presence suffused Buddhist and Hindu cultures of the past and, indeed, our own culture in medieval times, but the post-enlightenment world in the west has turned increasingly towards naturalism and technology and the same trends seem to be extending into the rest of the world at a rapid rate. The fact that some modern societies are democratic, while an increasing number are totalitarian, may not be as significant in the long run as the absence of the divine dimension in human experience. It may well be that the absence of a sense of divine presence may account for the increase in the rise of totalitarian regimes of both the right and the left. When the gods of religion have fled, the gods of the state and the party come in to fill the vacuum.

As world cultures become dominated by technology, the possibilities of self-indulgence and self-gratification opened up by that technology become more alluring. It seems a worthwhile task in the midst of these times to ask if the "still small voice" of divine presence still manifests itself in human experience. Perhaps the departure of the divine dimension in human experience is not as obvious as it appears to be at first. Can God still appear in the whirlwind or in the burning bush?

It may seem strange in this day and age to talk about "givenness," let alone divine "givenness." Most philosophers are aware of the attack against foundationalism in epistemology and of the destruction of the myth of the given. Any talk of givenness seems strangely out of fashion and recalls echoes of old philosophical debates of the thirties, forties and fifties. It is apparent that all knowledge claims involve an interpretive matrix. There is no basic bedrock from which everything starts and on which everything else can be built. Nevertheless, in the contemporary haste to do away with foundationalism, we may tend to forget that humans do confront a world even while they are interpreting it. We may indeed build worlds, as Goodman has maintained, but we do not build them out of thin air alone. While all knowledge involves interpretive frameworks and while there are no frameworks that have the particularly favored status of showing us how "things really are," it does not follow that the worlds of our concern are pure fabrications.

We are in the worlds of our concern and interpret how you will, <u>impingement</u> on consciousness by something outside of consciousness does occur and this impingement can reasonably be referred to as the <u>given</u> aspect in experience--not the pure given, to be sure, but an interpreted given nonetheless. Peirce was quite aware that there is no uninterpreted given but he also felt that givenness of some kind does occur. What I mean by something given is something that confronts us in our experience which we do not think we imagine or invent and which we take to be external to the self. In a perfectly ordinary way we take such things as chairs, automobiles, houses and trees to be given, and on reflection we do not take hallucinations and dreams to be given in this sense, because they are not thought to be part of the external world. Dreams are given in a more restricted sense. Dreams make a strong impingement on consciousness, but they have no public character--they are not shared by others.

I propose using the term "divinity" as a generic term to designate those experiences where an aspect of givenness occurs to which one could attach some religious significance. These experiences most often occur within the context of some kind of religious community, but as we shall see, they may include experiences that occur outside the context of any religious tradition. This is a fairly wide spectrum of experiences, to be sure, but most experiences do not involve divine givenness in any remarkably noteworthy sense, hence we are speaking about a restricted set of human experiences.

The nearest thing to a common denominator for what I am calling experiences of divine givenness would be impingement on consciousness from outside the self by aspects of the world that enhance human value and/or indicate that the universe is supportive of human efforts at enhancing value. This is admittedly vague, but we are talking about intimations of divinity, and intimations are vague. Usage of the term "divinity" also precludes describing religious experiences in terms of a particular religious tradition to the exclusion of other traditions. We will occasionally talk about the existence of God or the givenness of God, but such language puts you within the narrower framework of theistic religions. As long as one keeps the distinction between "divinity" and "God" in mind, no harm is done.[1] Talk about "God" also implies that some kind of religious "object" is given. In our discussion we do not want to presuppose this; hence, the vaguer term, "divinity," seems preferable. No matter what kind of philosophical perspective you embrace, divinity poses problems for philosophers in a sense in which the existence of chairs and persons poses no such problem. In discussing experiences of divine givenness I want to take as my base of departure the existence of things and persons, which are characterized predominately by some kind of givenness in the public domain.

It is patently obvious that if divinity appears, such appearance does not fall under the model of the appearance of existent objects. From a naturalistic perspective there is no divinity because divinity lacks the requisites for existence in the sense of givenness we have been talking about so far. While fully recognizing that divinity is radically different from things and persons, religious believers nevertheless insist that divine presence occurs too. While the presence of divinity is bound to be radically different from the presence of things and persons, if one is to seriously support the idea of divine presence in any religiously significant sense, then such divinity must be partially <u>given</u>, though this givenness, too, will be different from that of our base paradigm.

Confrontation and impingement on consciousness is an essential factor of givenness. Interpret it how you will, I confront a thing or a person as something or someone I have to deal with or at least acknowledge. The crucial aspect of existence for our purposes lies in the idea of direct givenness in experience. We might say that to establish the existence of anything or anybody empirically is to maintain that such things are given in a public manner.

Unless you are going to fall back on revelation or proof, the religious believer is going to have to opt for some kind of divine givenness. Clearly, such givenness will be different from what we have called givenness so far, and whether the notion makes sense as applied to divinity is highly questionable, but I would like to explore the possibility that it does make sense. The most persuasive reason for taking divine givenness seriously comes from surveying the vast amount of data concerning religious and mystical experiences. The accumulated data in this area is massive. The outstanding characteristic of mystical reports seems to be impingement on consciousness of some kind of larger consciousness, as James cautiously puts it. There would be no point in taking the epistemic claims of religion seriously if it were not for the reports of religious experiences. Most religious people are not mystics, but without reports of religious experiences religion could be adequately dealt with in reductionist sociological terms. Even so, it is still possible to interpret these experiences in terms of social conditioning, wish fulfillment and father image projection. To do so, however, would be to take too cavalier an attitude towards the data, but clearly this is a live option.

What makes religious experiences noteworthy is the aspect of givenness in the reports that mystics make. There is reason to be cautious, however. Many have overemphasized the similarities in the reports of the mystics and have not paid sufficient attention to the differences. One is tempted to over-stress the similarities in the reports, for to do so seems to give the requisite public character to reports of the divine givenness. To put it bluntly, if all mystics report the same thing in their experiences, then the divine givenness seems closer to the givenness of things and persons.

There are, however, significant differences in the reports as well as similarities, as anyone reading the literature can discover for himself. We are dealing here with the obvious fact that any kind of givenness is also an interpreted givenness. Buddhist, Hindu and Christian categories and theologies are quite diverse. It is not at all clear, given the reports of the mystics, that there always is necessarily a divine "object" that impinges on consciousness. Impingement on consciousness there seems to be, but impingement of what? The Jew and the Christian will talk about the impingement of God--a discrete theistic entity of some kind, characterized as Person. For a Hindu, Buddhist or nature mystic, nothing like this may be reported at all. For many, religious experience is a particular way of experiencing the rest of the world. As John Smith has said, religious experiences seem to be experiences of something else at the same time. If we wish to speak of the existence of a personal God, based on the givenness of divinity, it looks as though we will have to restrict ourselves to those who interpret these experiences in theistic terms. One could make a strong argument that religious experiences are simply a rather fine and exalted way of looking at the rest of the world, the world of things and persons that are given. The theist might respond that the diversity in the reports of the mystics is not damaging, for even in reporting the objects of everyday life, radically different conceptual schemes have been used. So, the theist might respond, diversity of conceptual schemes when it comes to describing the divine does not rule out there being an element of divine givenness, describe it how you will.

Nevertheless, for large numbers of persons throughout the world, including many who would call themselves religious, there is no divine givenness in any sense or under any linguistic description. For many Christians and Jews, God is believed in on the basis of faith, and to think that he might be given to the believer would be considered blasphemous and false. For many, it is precisely the absence of divine givenness that makes faith crucial.

The diversity of description, the element of faith, and

the unimportance of givenness for many believers would seem to doom our attempt to deal with divine givenness. Nevertheless, there are still promising possibilities, but the difficulties just mentioned are real. If religious faith were based totally on revealed doctrine and church dogma alone, religion could be written off as childlike superstition that should be grown out of by mature adults in the twentieth century. With all its diversity, the richness and wealth found in mystical literature precludes such a simple dismissal. While far from universal, the widespread actuality of religious and mystical experience indicates it is reasonable to entertain the idea of some kind of divine givenness. How to characterize it, given the relativity of interpretations, is what is most difficult. We have already seen that _phenomenologically_ divine givenness occurs, but to draw strong metaphysical conclusions from this is something else and is epistemically quite risky.

A happy way to characterize divine givenness is to speak of it in terms of what we might call intimations of divinity. Peter Berger is making the same point in the title of his book _A Rumor of Angels_.[2] What is indicated by rumors and intimations is the weak epistemic force of divine givenness as compared with that of things and persons, but, though weak, the epistemic force is not nil. Granted the element of the subjective interpretation, some common phenomenological features of divine givenness can be indicated. What James calls a sense of continuity with some kind of benevolent consciousness larger than our own seems to be a striking feature of divine givenness. Direct encounter with a personal God of the western theistic tradition does not seem to be a common feature, however, and this is a major stumbling block to establishing the existence of a personal God through divine givenness. Hindus, Buddhists, and various kinds of nature mystics do not necessarily characterize their religious experiences in western theistic categories. What does seem common to both eastern and western mysticism is the sense of some kind of union with a larger source of <u>value</u> which can be spoken of either in terms of a larger consciousness and/or a feeling that the universe is receptive in some sense to the enhancement of human value experiences. It is felt that the universe is in some sense basically good, rather than evil or value neutral. This is admittedly vague and imprecise, but when one is dealing with intimations, precision is simply not to be had.

Our concern is with features presented in the experience which one simply confronts, no matter how else the experience gets interpreted. A sense of value support is a strong feature of such experiences. A Christian like Augustine speaks of it in theistic categories as support from the "everlasting arms of God." Various other descriptions inside and outside the Christian tradition will speak of an enhanced sense of joy and well being even in the face of great adversity. The intensity and beauty of everyday things in experience is often reported as is a sense or "feel for" the unity of all things together. I hasten to add that what I am talking about here is a "feel for" the givenness of the unity of all things in some kind of a value complex, and not primarily an intellectual belief. Such "raw feels" manifest qualitatively divine Firstness using Peirce's category. An intellectual belief system may be inferred from this "raw feel" but I am not concerned with the belief but only with the given feeling of unity within the world and of value enhancement. At times the impingement of a larger source of value is so strong that the self feels that its own center of ego consciousness dissolves or is absorbed in the larger consciousness. This is givenness in a very strong sense, but it still lacks the public aspect of givenness, hence a dramatic religious experience with maximum impact on an individual could still be interpreted as similar to an hallucination.

Public character is precisely the problem at the heart of divine givenness. The impact of such givenness on many is obvious, but its apparent private character makes it quite reasonable for one to interpret such experiences as hallucinatory. Phenomenologically there is clearly an impact that seems to come from outside the self but whether one should attach any ontological weight to this or not is debatable. One can interpret divine givenness as a real impact of a larger consciousness on our own, but one can also give a reasonable interpretation for regarding divine givenness as hallucinatory in nature, indicating something interesting about human psychology, but implying nothing about a larger consciousness outside the self. As is increasingly recognized there is no _absolute_ conceptual framework in philosophy which would tell us which interpretation _must be_ chosen. Experience always remains ambiguous and open for multiple interpretations.

Let us assume for our purpose that divine givenness, as reported by mystics in different cultures, has some epistemic force and suppose one is inclined to entertain the possibility that some kind of divine consciousness larger than our own is presented to persons. What does this tell us about the existence of _God_? When we talk about God, we are usually talking about the object of belief in western theism and more specifically we are talking about a _personal_ God. It is quite a jump from divine givenness of some kind or other to a personal God. The whole context of western prayer and devotion would make no sense whatsoever if God were not conceived of as personal. While we have indicated that many reports of divine givenness do not seem to involve a personal God, clearly, many other reports _do_ involve what is taken to be a relation to a personal God. Thus, within the range of reports of divine givenness, there is a subclass of such reports that describe the divine givenness in terms of relation to a personal God.

It is this subclass of reports that serves as our basic data when it comes to talking about the existence of _God_. It must be fully recognized that reports of experience of God clearly reflect the categories of interpretation of western theism. The culturally conditioned interpretive categories are always operative in any experience, but it does not necessarily follow from this observation that there is no personalistic given component external to the self to be interpreted. Granted the private character of divine givenness, it still does not necessarily follow that all such experiences must be classified as hallucinatory. Nevertheless, reports of experiences of God are epistemically suspect for quite good reasons.

Though there are reports of direct presentation of God, there is a strong historical tradition that one cannot see God and live, as well as many references to the _hiddenness_ of God. If God is hidden, or if God is disclosed only in events and things of the world, then doesn't this imply that God can only be reached by a process of _inference_ from empirical data, and, thus, the thesis that God can be given would be refuted? In answering we must keep some important distinctions in mind. I have argued that some kind of divine impact or givenness can be recognized, granting that the interpretation of such givenness is culturally conditioned and, thus, relative. John Smith makes a distinction by saying that God is revealed through a historical medium _directly_ but not _immediately_.[3] By means of this distinction, he seeks to differentiate his view from that which derives God by a process of inference, or one which receives God immediately. Thus, one could avoid total divine _immediacy_ on the one hand, and avoid God as the end of a process of rational inference on the other hand.

In explicating this notion of direct but not immediate

experience, Smith takes our knowledge of the <u>self</u> to be the paradigm case to work with. Persons are both disclosed and hidden at the same time. I know you directly without a process of inference being necessary, but I don't have immediate access to you, for much is hidden from me. Nevertheless, impingement of you on my consciousness does occur. Smith suggests that our awareness of God would be something like our awareness of other persons. Unfortunately for the analogy, other persons possess bodies which are publicly observable and physical in the strongest sense. God may indeed be revealed or disclosed in physical things and events, but he is not disclosed unambiguously as a person is disclosed in his or her own body. It is because of embodiment that we can say, "See that person sitting over there?" or point directly to other persons. One may want to say, "Can't you see God in this situation?", but to point directly to him will not work due to the highly ambiguous way in which God appears.

One of the main difficulties is that God, unlike people and things, generally is not apprehended outside the context of a prior faith. It is widely held that God is not to be approached objectively or from a spectator view of knowledge, but approached with a faith and belief that is present to the believer <u>prior</u> to apprehension of God. This often is the case but it is one of the main difficulties when dealing with divine givenness and considerably weakens the epistemic force of religious knowledge claims. Still, one might want to argue that <u>within</u> a given faith context, one believer may say to another that he can see the disclosure of God in a particular event or situation. Unfortunately, it is also the case that people often have strong disagreements as to where God is disclosing himself, even though they share the same faith context. Divine embodiment, like human embodiment, would make things much easier but even though we grant that God is disclosed in things and events, a basic ambiguity always remains as to where and when God is disclosed.

Smith suggests that divine disclosure occurs mainly through <u>holy persons, historical occasions</u> and <u>the order and arrangement of nature</u>. At least he sees these as crucial aspects of divine disclosure in the Hebraic tradition. The Christian tradition adds another and for Christians the most important disclosure--that through the God-person of the Christ. For them, it seems, you could at least have an unambiguous divine embodiment.

From within a given faith context this seems to be an accurate portrayal of the situation, but viewed philosophically and outside the faith context, ambiguity abounds. In one sense holy persons, historical occasions, the order of nature and Jesus have been given in a more or less straight-forward way, but to see these as cases of divine disclosure involves a strong interpretive element based on faith. When I say interpretive element I do not mean that divinity is necessarily inferred from these presentations. Smith is right about the directness of the disclosure--for the believer there is a direct but not immediate disclosure of God. Although direct and disclosed, an interpretive element surely is involved. Each of these phenomena,however, can be read in different ways. For the non-Christian, Jesus is just another man, though admittedly a very unusual one. The most that philosophy can do is admit the possibility of divine disclosure, while insisting on the intrinsic ambiguity involved in such disclosure.

Let us look at some possibilities of divine disclosure that might occur in _ordinary_ experiences and which do not involve entering the faith commitment of a particular religious tradition. While most instances of divine disclosure occur within the circle of a given faith community, it would seem that such events should also occur outside of a given faith community. If divinity can appear in the world at all, it would seem that such appearances would not be restricted to particular religious communities. It has been said that God does not disclose himself to persons who have not prepared themselves for such disclosure by discipline, prayer, fasting and meditation, preferably within the context of some religious community. While true in the most apparent cases of divine disclosure it does not follow that all disclosures must occur within conventionally established religious contexts. Also, within a religious community where theistic categories are part of the conditioning factors on the believer, the reports of divine encounter may be more epistemically suspect than where such reports occur outside of the conditioning factors of a faith community.

If what I am calling intimations of divinity occurred only within religious communities, one might suspect that all such reports were simply the product of strong social conditioning. Reports that occur outside of religious communities are possibly more noteworthy than reports within religious communities when it comes to examining divine givenness. Furthermore, if we can uncover experiences which are common to most people, not just to mystics, and which could reasonably be taken as examples of divine disclosure, this would be even more striking. What we would be looking for would be experiences which could be described as direct but not immediate encounters with divinity where what we mean by "direct" is that divinity is not derived by a process of inference.

One of the most promising investigations in this area is seen in Berger's fascinating book, A Rumor of Angels. Therein he coins the happy phrase, signals of transcendence,[4] which I would take to be similar to what I am calling intimations of divinity. These signals manifest themselves in experiences common to everyone, in or outside of religious traditions, which can be taken as signals of transcendence or intimations of divine disclosure. One example Berger mentions is a sense of trust in the universe expressed in such statements as "everything will be all right" which we tell each other in times of stress, tragedy and need. Berger makes the interesting observation that if we treated such remarks as ordinary empirical statements of fact or as predictions they would be patently false in many instances. That, however, is not their primary intent, nor does the logic of such statements operate in the ordinary way. Berger says that when we comfort another person in such terms, we are expressing a deep gut level trust in the goodness of the universe. Without such a deep level trust life could scarcely be lived for we would be sunk in such a paranoid level of distrust and suspicion of the universe that little if anything could be accomplished.

Berger's point is that this phenomenon can be taken as a signal of transcendence, and by a signal, he does not mean that it provides any kind of proof for God or any reasonably strong inference to divinity. The epistemic force of such a signal is weak, but Berger feels that it can be taken as a signal of a transcendent source of value--that a direct but not immediate disclosure of divinity occurs. It is a suggestive idea. Admittedly, the signal, if it is one, is extremely weak. It would never occur to most of us to take our trust in the universe, expressed in comforting others, as a signal of a direct encounter with God or a signal of transcendence. Even when this possibility has been pointed out to us, it may seem to be "clutching at straws" to take such trust as a signal of transcendence, let alone presentation of a personal God. One might well argue at this point that there is considerable difference between a signal of transcendence or an intimation of divinity and the givenness of God, even if direct experience of God is also experience of something else as well. After all, smoke is a signal or sign of fire, but seeing smoke does not entail that one also sees the fire at the same time. Much hinges here on the notion of what one means by direct apprehension. It makes perfectly good sense to say, "I see there is a fire over there" when all I actually see is the smoke. In the examples given by both John Smith and Peter Berger one can make a case that the examples they mention may be taken as signals of transcendence if one so chooses. John Smith argues that his examples can also be taken as direct experiences of divinity, at least by those within the Jewish and Christian traditions.

It is one thing to infer the designer God of the teleological argument from the order and arrangement of nature. It is something else again to "see" God directly in the order and arrangement of nature. The latter is a feature of much religious life and experience; the former is a rational procedure engaged in by theologians and philosophers. The impingement on consciousness of the order and arrangement of nature can be taken as also the direct impingement of God on consciousness. This is perfectly compatible with the fact that for many others the order and arrangement of nature is not taken as an impingement of the divine on consciousness. When we tell somebody that "everything will be all right," we certainly do not have to interpret this in any religious way whatsoever. But in the act of trust and faith, the sensitive and acute observer could also maintain that God or divinity impinges on consciousness.

Plato may be helpful in our discussion at this point. I am not concerned here with the metaphysics that Plato constructs to explain signals of transcendence. I am interested that he noticed such signals in human experience and stressed them more than most other thinkers. Plato noticed and made much of the fact that human beings are ill adapted for everyday life in the empirical world. It is notorious that we are proverbially discontent. Provide us with the necessities of life and we become bored and restless--we develop neuroses, search for meaningful careers and ask about the meaning of life. Not all of us do this in an obvious way and the degree of unrest varies widely. Still, a human being who enjoys nothing but eating, drinking and sex, who has no hobbies, no career interest or concerns outside his own self-gratification will be continually restless and unhappy. He will find life continually stupid and pointless and will try to escape through various forms of self-indulgence with which he is familiar. There is no question that without the necessities of life and without money, most of us are in bad shape, but what is interesting is that there is no evidence that those with wealth and power are intrinsically happier than the rest of us if all they have is wealth and power. If humans were geared for this life alone these situations should not occur. As far as we know, animals when surfeited with food and sex do not lapse into boredom, do not question the nature of their existence or worry about the meaning of life or look for something important to do. As far as we can tell, they <u>are</u> geared to this world, and the world is geared to satisfying their needs pretty well. Not so with humans. Perhaps it is no accident that this human discontent has sometimes been called divine discontent.

Plato was sensitive to the signals of transcendence when he referred to the body as the prison house of the soul. Kant too was aware of them when he suggested that since the world was so ill-suited to fulfill human happiness, that perhaps the universe had other purposes in mind for man, such as developing the morally good will. It is on the basis of such data that Plato and others have constructed their vast metaphysical systems. Since humans confront a given world that is so unsatisfactory, this deficiency could be taken as an intimation, not only of immortality, but of divinity as well. Another noteworthy aspect is the urge of various people to set projects and goals for themselves that they may never achieve, which may involve considerable sacrifice, including illness and death. These goals they set for themselves are often not required of them by others, and others may even look down on them and regard the pursuit of these goals as absurd. This may not be a usual mode of human behavior, but it is by no means rare and is considerably more common than mystical experience. The urge to human transcendence beyond what this world offers or demands of one may also be taken as a signal of transcendence. It should be kept in mind that the urge to transcendence does not necessarily mean a denial of this world, though often the pursuit of transcendence does involve the denial of the world in varying degrees.

There is no logical necessity to regard the body as the prison house of the soul. Happily the best of both worlds is often pursued. Part of the given of the human condition is the inadequacy of food, drink and shelter alone to provide a significant life. The givenness here is a lack or deficiency rather than a presence, but the givenness of the deficiency of the world is widespread enough to be noteworthy. And this lack occurs inside and outside the contexts of organized religion. The felt lack varies among human beings and many would report no consciousness of such a lack, but it seems likely that where the lack is not felt or if felt, not responded to, life will tend to sink into routine boredom at best.

It is in the area of moral experience more than anywhere else that the givenness of signals of transcendence may point towards divinity. Plato was vividly aware of this as were many others. Setting aside Platonic metaphysics, humans do seem to apprehend standards of moral perfection, goodness and justice which never were and never will be empirically exemplified. These can be explained in naturalistic terms as simple projections from the self, but since naturalism is no more a privileged stance than any other, one can also opt to take the possession of such moral standards in consciousness as direct intimations of divinity. Given a purely reductionistic view of ethics, one wonders how to account for the fact that cultures have been found radically morally deficient by individuals who spoke out against cultural conventions. If morality is simply a product of social conditioning, how is it that time and again in the history of the world, individuals have brought society into question and have judged society morally deficient? One is at liberty to wonder if the rejection of human slavery, the growing rejection of racism, sexism and war does not represent the gentle impingement of divinity on the groping human consciousness. Again one is not forced to this conclusion by logic or experience, but the gentle proddings of experience may be worth more notice than has generally been the case. Moral outrage against acts that fall beyond the pale is another of the signals of transcendence. Berger deals at some length with moral outrage as a signal.

Moral experience and moral outrage are experiences common to the mass of persons at one time or other, inside and outside religious traditions, and thus may be taken as transcendent signals. These signals, often gentle, but by no means always so, confront us with our moral deficiencies and lure us to be better than we are.

Let us combine the notions of a signal, sign or intimation to that of direct givenness. To do so one would have to say that it makes sense to say, "I see there is a fire over there" when all I immediately perceive is the smoke which I take as a sign of fire, and it is not straining things too much to say that fire is directly given. If it is legitimate in this case, it should be legitimate for a person to say, "I see God in the order and arrangement of nature." The main difference is that the epistemic force of the fire example is much stronger than the God example. In the case of fire we do not speak of intimations of fire but simply of seeing the fire. While we do speak of intimations of divinity, we can also describe it as direct awareness of divinity.

Assuming a difference of degree rather than kind in our apprehension of fire and divinity, the degree is still wide and the epistemic force is weak in the case of the divine. I have spoken of epistemic force before, but something more must be said explicitly about it. The existence of things and persons has reasonably strong epistemic force. We do not have to construct ingenious arguments to establish the existence of things and persons the way we do when we deal with God or with theoretical entities in science. I am aware that the existence of the external world has been a persistent philosophical problem for centuries, but that is just the point--it has been a philosopher's problem, debated in the esoteric corridors of academe, while the existence of God has been an anguishing existential and religious problem for many ordinary people, as well as an esoteric philosophical problem. As Hume was only too painfully aware, outside the academic halls the impingement of the external world is obvious enough, even to philosophers. This is increasingly recognized even within the halls of academic philosophy in our own time, with the general rejection of the spectator theory of knowledge. Coupled with this is rejection of the Cartesian assumption that we are imprisoned within self-consciousness and somehow have to "climb out" of consciousness to the external world. Most schools of contemporary philosophy take it for granted that we are already "in the world." Thus, the so-called problem of the external world seems increasingly to be a relic of past philosophical presuppositions. The problem of divinity, however, remains a significant one within the philosophical community as well as a problem for much of the general public.

Within strongly oriented religious and mystical communities, or in great ages of faith it may seem strange to speak of divinity in such epistemically weak terms, but in our age this stance seems appropriate. In wide segments of contemporary culture the divine dimension of experience is eclipsed or absent altogether. Only the strong in faith or those deeply committed to a particular revelation will escape the ambiguities mentioned here and then only through a volitional act of will. Of course, religious people have always claimed that this is what is required. However, granting the epistemic weakness of the intimations, the signals of transcendence are there. In the case of things and persons we are talking about "evidence and proof." These terms are epistemically inappropriate in dealing with divinity. Here we must speak of "faith," "intimation" and remote "symbols."

Impingement of the divine on consciousness is a distinct possibility and in western theistic terms we may refer to this as the givenness of God. This much at least seems required unless one is going to throw out all reports of mystical and religious experience as delusory. Dramatic and important as the reports of the mystics are, of even more importance are the signals of transcendence mentioned by Berger, for these refer to the common experiences of all of us; if divinity is given at all, it would seem peculiar if such experiences were had only by full blown mystics. While all the data taken together make a reasonable case for divine impingement, religious empiricists may have paid too much attention to dramatic mystical encounters and not enough to the "still small voice" that may ever so gently impinge on consciousness. Whitehead's metaphysics of a persuasive God who acts as a "lure" is probably the most significant contemporary *philosophical* justification for taking gentle signals of transcendence seriously.

We saw earlier that the divine component is radically lacking in the mode of Thirdness--that lawlike behavior on the part of God is more or less absent. Some would argue that this is not so. Mystics have argued that strict and continuous meditation and worship techniques can produce a continuing sense of the presence of the divine. They have argued that the apparent unpredictability of religious experience is due to the failure to discipline oneself, to put oneself in the frame of mind where divinity can be present. Certainly the importance of disciplined meditation cannot be overlooked but the absence of divine Thirdness is still noteworthy. There have been reports of sudden religious conversions of persons who have made no preparations for it and who have frequently been strongly anti-religious up to the moment of their conversion. More importantly most people cannot and will not engage in disciplined meditation, and many who try to lead the religious life do not succeed in their religious quest. Dedicated mystics themselves report the experience of the "dark night of the soul" where God is absent and withdrawn. There is something peculiar about telling people who are unable to achieve religious enlightenment that it is because they did not try hard enough, or tried too hard, or failed to do something else. A Biblical scholar of my acquaintance once told me that a lot has been written about the presence of God, but not nearly enough about the *absence* of God. In this connection it is interesting to note the parables of Jesus that refer to the absent master, not absent permanently to be sure, but absent nevertheless.

Following Peirce's terminology, I would say that divinity may exist, but is not real, for reality is Thirdness. For Peirce, laws of nature are real but they do not exist. To say that divinity exists but may not be real sounds bizarre when put this way but given the technical use of these terms it well may be the case. Most of the time we are content to use the terms "existence" and "reality" interchangeably, but in the interests of philosophical precision we might say that the divine may well exist but is not real, meaning by "real" only that experience of the divine cannot be subsumed under lawlike rules. This seems odd, nevertheless, for it would seem to put divinity in the same categorical classification as dreams and hallucinations--strong degrees of Firstness and Secondness, but minimal or no Thirdness. There is a difference here that should be kept in mind. Dreams and hallucinations are intrinsically private to the persons who have them, but divinity seems to have a quasi-public aspect. As we have already seen, divinity lacks the public aspect of things and persons, but there are interesting similarities that run through the reports of the mystics. Though these must not be overestimated as we saw earlier, they are worth noting and have been pointed out again and again by James and other writers on religious experience. Thus, there is a quasi-public character to religious experience that binds mystics from different religious traditions together. Also there seem to be group experiences of divinity such as can occur in a Quaker meeting or in other religious groups as well. Beyond this, Berger's signals of transcendence are shared by most, even if not attributed to divinity, thus again giving a quasi-public aspect to such signals.

Such experiences are not lawlike--one can never tell when the "spirit" will descend into a Quaker meeting, but they do have a quasi-public character that differentiates them from the purely private cases of Secondness involved in dreams and hallucinations. While religious experiences do have some epistemic force, nevertheless, dreams, hallucinations and divinity would share in common presentations of Secondness but not Thirdness. In Peirce's technical sense divinity could be characterized as existent but not real. In the different sense in which what is "real" is what is of supreme value, divinity would indeed be real. Once the ambiguities in the term "real" are recognized, our usage appears less odd. Though lacking in Thirdness, the quasi-public aspect of many religious experiences serves to differentiate them from dreams and hallucinations. Drawing on Peirce again, another use of the term "reality" should be noted. Peirce also spoke of the real as being that which holds independently of what you, I or anyone else in particular think to be the case. In <u>this</u> sense, divinity might be considered as real. All in all, the paradigm case of what is real and existent in the strong sense would still be things and persons. Divinity departs from this strong paradigm. Hence we can only speak of intimations of divinity, given an empiricist perspective, and similarly we do not speak of intimations of things and persons.

One further aspect of the topic of divine givenness should be noted. Many people believe in God by instinct, and by instinct I mean not an intellectually articulated belief, but a gut level feeling. This is related to the "raw feel" of an orderly universe that we spoke of earlier. When all is said and done, many feel that some kind of divinity lies at the heart of things. This too could be taken as a signal of transcendence, subject to all the ambiguities of the other signals we have looked at. Peirce thought that what we believe on instinct about values is basically sound because the mind is attuned to nature. The instinct for belief in God as a signal of transcendence was certainly more widespread in the nineteenth century than it is now. As a signal it was widespread--its quasi-public aspect was apparent, and, thus, it was an important aspect to notice when talking about divine givenness.

In our time this signal has been considerably diminished in power, but is by no means absent altogether. The secularization of human life throughout the world is increasingly obvious. Regardless of what is officially professed, human societies increasingly operate as though there were no divine dimension whatsoever. India with its long historical religious tradition is only one example. In functional operating terms, the legacy of Gandhi appears to be dead. India is increasingly just as militaristic and technologically oriented as most other countries. What people throughout the world increasingly want is a life of leisure and enjoyment made available to us through the magic of technology. This can be combined and often is combined with continuing awareness of the divine dimension of experience, but it doesn't take much effort to see the growing feelings of emptiness and alienation of large numbers of people, particularly in highly industrialized technological cultures. This trend was noted by Kierkegaard and Nietzsche in the nineteenth century and was stressed again more strongly by Heidegger in the twentieth century.

It is an open question whether the deep instinct for the divine dimension is as pervasive now as Peirce perceived it to be in the last century. Even at that time, Nietzsche read human experience quite differently from Peirce. This signal of transcendence has dimmed and in the withdrawal of the gods, the vacancy is filled by the growing desire to reap the fruits of enjoyment produced by technology. It would be going too far to maintain that the instinct for divinity is dead or will ever die. This signal of transcendence is still there and may re-emerge more strongly in the future, but for the present, its force is considerably diminished. The gods may have fled for now, but who knows how or when they may return? In speaking of the givenness of divinity, this signal, though diminished in strength, must still be noticed.

NOTES

[1] See Chapter 10.

[2] Peter L. Berger, _A Rumor of Angels_ (Garden City, N.Y.: Doubleday Anchor, 1970).

3 John E. Smith, _Experience and God_ (New York: Oxford University Press, 1968) p. 83.

[4] Berger, _op. cit._, p. 52.

CHAPTER 10

"DIVINITY" AND "GOD" AS PHILOSOPHICAL CATEGORIES

In this chapter I want to explain and develop important features of two concepts, that of "divinity" and that of "God." The intent is to stress the distinction between phenomenological and ontological considerations, taking "divinity" to be primarily a phenomenological category and "God" to be one that involves explicit ontological commitment. As a phenomenological category, "divinity" will refer to various aspects of human experience that can be interpreted as having reference beyond the individual self or community of selves to a source of value and religious significance that transcends human communities. When this source of value and significance is explicitly worshipped as a personal being then we are dealing with the concept of "God." I would suggest that the use of "God" involves an intent to refer to an "object" though admittedly an "object" of a very special sort. All I mean by "object" here is that explicit <u>ontological commitment</u> is involved in the use of the term "God."

My use of the term "divinity" implies no such ontological commitment, but does indicate a phenomenological experience which can be characterized as <u>impingement</u> on consciousness of some kind of larger source of value or larger consciousness. While experiences interpreted as fraught with divine significance tend to be taken ontologically by many, for my purposes here no more is intended than that the experience is interpreted as or <u>felt to be</u> the impingement of a larger source of value on my own consciousness--an experience with religious significance. Whether such experiences are to be interpreted as delusory or as fraught with ontological significance makes no difference to the phenomenological character of the experience.

Let us take an example. The urge to create and to excel in some area of human endeavor covers a very wide territory but certain features can be noted which are of importance. The cases that are relevant to our study are those where the person involved feels a strong urge to achieve something even in the face of great obstacles or in spite of strong inclinations not to pursue the creative activity involved. In these situations the creative activity involved is pursued more or less with a "sense of mission" that seems to come from outside the self and often seems to "fly in the face" of what the self wants to do or what seems rational and sensible. Not all acts of creative endeavor have this feature, but my concern is only with those situations where such factors are present.

In such situations one feels as if "compelled" to carry out the activity, and while one may take deep personal satisfaction in the results, there is often the feeling that one did not produce the results completely on the basis of one's own efforts alone. The person feels more like a <u>conduit</u>, transmitting creative expression rather than a creator of value from within the self. This feeling of "compulsion" can range from the forceful, where one feels fully under the weight of such compulsion, to the very weak, where one simply finds oneself often doing things that are not required by the immediate situation and even where one would rather be doing something else instead. The artist creating a picture and dissatisfied until he gets it "just right," the scientific researcher or military strategist who tries to "tie up all the loose ends" and works far in excess of what the empirical situation might call for, are examples of this type of inner compulsion. The compulsion of the "workaholic" might often be a similar case in point, but in some cases such as this the compulsion is often negatively motivated in the sense that the "workaholic" may simply drive himself at work because he is running away from problems at home. In the same person, both negative and positive factors may be at work simultaneously. It is the positive factor that is of concern to us and clearly there are cases where one feels a creative urge that is positive and is not adequately explained simply as an attempt "to get away from something else." Are these urges unconsciously motivated then? Possibly, but one is also entitled to take such creative events as examples of divine Secondness.

Why use "divinity" to describe what goes on here? I use it mainly because the creative impingement of the "other" is generally felt as a positive value force, as life enhancing for the artist and scientist and frequently as value enhancing for the larger community. In such situations it is often felt that the universe, so to speak, is "on our side" in this matter. To feel this way, I suggest, is to feel touched by divinity. Whitehead's "lure" to creativity captures some of what I have in mind except that Whitehead develops this notion in an ontological direction. It should be kept in mind that for many who feel this kind of creative compulsion, no explicit attribution of divinity may be involved at all; nevertheless, I want to suggest that "divinity" is an appropriate category when one feels that he alone is not the complete source of the creative urge.

What about the ethical implication of what has been said? If the urge to paint, to construct scientific theory, to build a better weapons system, to commit the perfect crime or build an efficient drug smuggling network could all involve "divinity," then this forces the term far beyond the reasonable bounds of legitimate explication, for part of what is generally meant by use of the term "divinity" is that it be applied in contexts where morality is not damaged and is possibly enhanced. One could argue that behind the impingement of divinity is always the "lure" to enhance human value, not only for the individual involved, but for the world community in general. In terms of the dyadic relationship involved, it might be that due to human finitude, if not perverseness, the morally bad creative act is always the result of blind or perverse human decision. It might well be that the compulsion felt by the sadist to inflict pain on others is a misinterpretation of the impingement of divinity. Here "impingement" is a better term than "compulsion" for the latter term gives the impression of no free choice. Let us say that the sadist freely chooses to inflict pain on his victim, misreading the impulse from divinity to achieve value enhancement in a more ethically acceptable way. It might be said that to introduce any kind of moral distinction at all at this level of analysis is to desert the level of phenomenological description, smuggling in one's own value presuppositions to the concept of "divinity." Maybe we should say that the creative urge manifests itself in various ways, or maybe divinity manifests itself by impingement in situations some of which we would call moral and some which we would call immoral. To stop here though does seem to involve stretching the concept of "divinity" beyond the bounds of reasonable explication. Perhaps all we can say is that divine impingement is always seen by the person involved as some kind of value _enhancement_, but that, tragically, persons are often prone to seek this value enhancement in terms of stupid and/or immoral choices. The creative urge may still be a divinely inspired urge even if it is responded to inappropriately. Whitehead captures the idea when he says that though the "lure" comes from God, the choice is ours.

This discussion leads us naturally into a second aspect of quiet impingement on consciousness and that is the direct impingement of the moral dimension or the _ought_. That the moral dimension may be an impingement of divinity on consciousness is, as we have seen, even more apparent than is the case with the creative urge in general, which is more open to ambiguous interpretation. Many people feel the moral dimension of experience lays an obligation on them to act or to refrain from acting in a certain way--it is no accident that Kant spoke of the moral dimension in terms of commands or laws which oblige us to act morally. It is true that he spoke of the moral law as self-given through reason rather than as externally given through revelation. While a command can be self-given and self-generated, phenomenologically, commands are much more suited to dyadic than monadic contexts. While A can give a command to A, the force of the term "command" generally implies that A gives a command to B, where A and B are not identical. This is so whether the context is a moral one or not. Experientially the moral "ought" is more frequently seen as coming from God or some kind of divine source. To maintain that the "ought" comes from God moves us outside the phenomenological realm to the realm of metaphysical commitment. Phenomenologically, all that can be said is that the concept of moral obligation grounded in what "ought to be" or "what ought not to be" <u>feels like</u> it is derived outside the self and often even outside the bounds of society. While one can easily interpret the "ought" impinging on the individual self in terms of socially conditioned norms, it is harder to account for the "ought" that condemns the very social structure itself. If all moral obligation were explainable in terms of the socializing and conditioning factors of society, why society itself is ever condemned would remain a mystery.

I have included morality under the category of quiet impingement as opposed to the dramatic encounters of the mystics, but this may need some qualification. For some of the Old Testament prophets, the command of the Lord to preach repentance was of a very dramatic nature, but I would suggest that the urge to moral betterment is more frequently heard as the "still small voice" of conscience. Furthermore, while moral conversion can be sudden and dramatic, less noticed, because less dramatic, is the slow growth in moral awareness and sensitivity that many people develop over a period of time. Many persons came slowly and painfully to the conclusion that owning persons as slaves was morally wrong and many are coming to the conclusion that discriminating against persons on the basis of race, or killing them in warfare is morally wrong. Human practices are not changed easily or quickly, for self-interest, custom and habit are strong and are very hard to overcome. Quietly, however, intimations of what I call the divine may impinge on our consciousness. The quiet sensitizing of more and more persons to the injustices perpetuated against minority groups and against nature in general also reflects such impingement.

Simple felt immediate pleasures and satisfactions probably do not in themselves involve disclosure of divinity. What marks experiences of divinity is a cumulative growth and development of the personality to greater levels of self-awareness and maturity. Included in this would be a deep and growing ethical sensitivity. Experiences of divinity tend to extend one's ethical concerns wider than that of the immediate family or nation. A person is better off in terms of maturity and awareness as a result of such experiences in the sense that there is a cumulative building of character in such experiences. Thus, a strong dispositional component is present--the tendency towards improvement. These kinds of value experiences are different from those experiences of value made up of various pleasures and immediate satisfactions which do not leave the person any better off than they were before they had the experiences.

Value experiences that do not enhance personal development may be perfectly real and important but would lack the qualification of divinity. There is no religious significance per se to eating a steak, drinking fine wine or listening to music, valuable as these are found to be, for one is not necessarily made better by having such experiences. Divinity characterizes those experiences where one feels "pushed" to be better than he is at present--where the urge to transcend oneself appears and where this urge is something more than being conditioned by others or by society to make the effort.

Plato spoke of such experiences involving the true, the good and the beautiful as ones where we are touched by the Ideal Forms. Such experiences make us feel that we are destined for something more than what ordinary empirical existence has to offer. If one switched to an ontologically "loaded" vocabulary one might speak of being touched by God or of residing in the world of Forms. That such self-transcendence occurs there can be no doubt, but one need make nothing more of it than seeing humans as having the peculiar capacity to set goals for themselves that go far beyond the simple ability to survive and live on the planet. Intimations of divinity occur as one comes to feel that he alone is not the sole inventor of his creative urges. In the final analysis my acts are mine and I am responsible for the outcome be it good or bad, but in certain of my acts I may come to feel what Whitehead calls the "lure" to choose in certain ways rather than in other ways. I may feel a certain sense of "leading" and "direction" for achieving value that comes from outside the self. Even if such leadings turn out to be delusive or fanciful, they would be marked by what I am calling the aspect of divinity. In the last analysis the term "divinity" implies no more nor less than that religious experiences occur which feel as though they involved impingement on my consciousness of a larger source of value than my own self can generate.

Let us now turn to considerations of "God" as a category. In explicating this concept it is essential to see "God" as an ontological category whereas "divinity" is a purely phenomenological category. When we apply the term "God" we imply a referent, some kind of religious "object" or "entity" though admittedly of a very special kind. A particularly important feature of God involves a personalistic aspect. Buber's I-Thou encounter between man and God is a classic paradigm of the man-God relation. When we talk about God we are talking about a personal God, meaning by this that God relates to man in a personal way, that one can address God through prayer in the I-Thou relationship.[1]

At this point let us stress that the whole context of theistic prayer and devotion presupposes a two term ontological relation between man and a personal God. When we talked about "divinity" we also spoke about a two term relation between man and divinity, but this was grounded _phenomenologically_ in felt impingement. With God, the two termed relation is explicitly _ontological_ whether impingement is present or not. What generally takes the place of experience is _faith_. Even if (experientially) only one term (man) is present, the believer must have faith that the other term of the relation is _real_ or has _being_ of some kind or other. "Divinity" is a manifestly empirical concept while the concept of "God" is not directly empirical in the same way.

When we speak of God, faith is the operative concept rather than experience. When we consider the concept of God philosophically it is essential that it have some _grounding_ in the empirical concept of divinity from which extrapolation can then be made to God. Without some empirical grounding, the concept of God would appear to be everything that Freud, Marx and other reductionist critics have said that it is.[2] While large numbers of people may not have experiences that could be characterized as impingement of divinity, the fact that many other persons _do_ have such experiences serves as a legitimate basis for extrapolation to belief in God. When we make this move towards belief, the culturally conditioned religious categories of expression come into play. Since "God" is such a culturally conditioned category, experience of divinity is often interpreted as an I-Thou personal relation, hence providing some basis for theistic extrapolation.

Even though God must be accorded a special and peculiar ontological status to make sense of asserting his existence in any sense at all, we must refer back to the empirical base of the phenomenological givenness of divinity. To go from the impingement of divinity to the existence of God does require a considerable chain of interpretation--from phenomenology to ontology. Still, the links in the chain must be there, for the only really compelling epistemic reason for asserting that there is a God is that divinity impinges on human consciousness.

Why bother making the distinction between divinity and God at all? Because from a phenomenological perspective, experiences of religious value impingement must be taken seriously. This means that when confronted by reports of religious experiences one should not automatically apply reductionist techniques to such reports, for to do so would be to violate the descriptive phenomenology involved. If experiences as reported <u>feel like</u> impingement on consciousness of a larger consciousness, it won't do "right off the bat" to say that such experiences are reducible to queer psychological states of the subject. In the interests of accurate description, purported experiences of divine impingement must be taken and reported as such experiences present themselves as being. When we move, on the other hand, to talk about God we are moving away from phenomenology into ontological commitment. Hence the distinction seems important to make.

In dealing with the concept of God, we cannot be indifferent to the question of God's being, primarily because religiously it is of the utmost importance. In some forms of extreme liberal protestantism there have been attempts to think of God as simply designating man's highest value impulses or ultimate concern, but religiously this "does not wash," nor is it plausible to interpret God as simply another term for social action and social justice. One does not have to be a fundamentalist Christian to see that for the mainstream of theism the <u>being of</u> God as entity is presupposed. Again the I-Thou encounter is the best paradigm to use for the theistic viewpoint and this presupposes that both the I and the Thou have real being, though the kind of being will differ radically between the self and God.

<u>Existence</u>, as applied to contingent beings or to God, is intrinsically mysterious and inexplicable rationally. Not only can we wonder why there is anything rather than nothing, we can also ask, as Kant did, whence then came God? Rationalists claim that it is an improper understanding that makes us ask how come there is a God? Yet any alert child asks it and from a purely logical viewpoint there does not seem any contradiction in wondering why there is God or in doubting his existence. Even though God and contingent beings would manifest themselves in radically different ways, there is

still basically a surd nonrational character to the existence of contingent beings and to the existence of God. It is not only religiously, but also philosophically, just as mysterious as to why there should be a God as to why there should be ordinary contingent beings. That God should exist at all is even more mysterious than that ordinary contingent beings exist, for at least we confront such contingent beings every day. While in one sense it may be a meaningless question to ask why anything should exist rather than nothing, it is nevertheless the case that there being anything at all remains a source of wonder and is ultimately inexplicable in the sense demanded by rationalism. The surd nonrational character of existence is something that rationalists have always rejected and which empiricists accept. Berkeley and other religious thinkers have regarded the very existence of the world as a miracle. I would add, the existence of God, if such be the case, would be a similar miracle.

As we said earlier, the existence of anything is a surd brute givenness of some kind. In a very profound sense, the existence of any contingent thing or of God is a _gift_, in a very special sense. From this perspective a gift is not always something we would like to receive, in fact it may not be desired at all, but it is a gift, nevertheless, in the sense that existence involves givenness in _presentation_ of some kind or other. It is true that gifts don't just spring out of thin air, but appear in a causal nexus, but as we saw earlier there is no logical necessity that there be anything at all, including a causal nexus or God. This is one reason why there is no answer to the question, why is there anything rather than nothing? The gift character of existence--the world and God simply appear, though in different ways. Sartre's description of the world as "de trop" approaches what we are talking about. From his own theological context Berkeley saw the issue clearly when he spoke of the existence of the world as a miracle--a literal gift from God. I am simply extending the "de trop" character of existence to God as well. The Anselmians would accept our characterization of existence as gift when applied to finite contingents, but would hold out for necessary existence for God, but in doing this they would destroy the important religious point that God himself is a gift to us of grace, not required by either experience or logic. Thus, religiously too, God's existence, if such there be, would be a gift of grace.

Thus, our result is that God too, if he exists, does not exist necessarily and requires some kind of world, as Whitehead indicates. Nevertheless, God would be a being with very special properties--the properties of love, ethical sensitivity and openness to all creatures. What is peculiar about this in ontological terms is that experience in the ordinary sense provides us with no <u>obvious</u> existent of this nature. Empirically, we remain at the level of divine impingement we spoke of earlier. From this we cannot infer that there is a God in any reasonably strong epistemic sense.

Is the believer justified in making such an extrapolation

from divinity? Is he justified in going from the phenomenological impingement of the divine to ontological commitment to the theistic God? In the "lifeworld" of religious faith and commitment, surely he is justified; this is done time and again and is basic to the religious life of theism. Of course, the believer himself does not make the transition in the way we have described; he simply has faith in God. Viewing it from a philosophical perspective, existentially, the believer's faith is justified. The extrapolation is partially justified epistemically because, as we saw earlier, divinity impinges on consciousness in various forms. Belief in God in not necessarily an irrational or childish act based on fear and superstition. Of course, once this is recognized it is apparent that there are a multiplicity of theistic doctrines about the nature of God--some highly incoherent and unethical, and other concepts more coherent with experience and science. Some concepts of God are also religiously inadequate and some more fully adequate; among the various theistic concepts a large element of speculation is involved. For the believer the givenness of divinity is in many cases immediately the givenness of God. For the believer, God may be present in the whirlwind, in the sunset and in the moral act. The interpretation of phenomenological divinity for the theist will be the direct presence of God in things and events. In the interpretation made by the theist, God is disclosed.

While disclosure of God can occur for the theist, it is

by no means always so, for there is a strong theistic tradition concerning the <u>hiddenness</u> of God. While God may be present in the communion of the I-Thou encounter, frequently in this relation only the human is present explicitly. For the believer, God is often hidden and absent--in fact this is probably more frequently the case than presence. In prayer, however, the believer has faith in the two term relation of I-Thou, for in prayer he reaches out to the "other." It is precisely the hiddenness and absence of God that generates the requirement of faith. The absence of God or the hiddenness of God is a marked aspect of religious life to many devout persons. In addition, modern technological culture throughout the world is increasingly secular in orientation, regardless of official lip service paid to religion.

For millions more, a purely naturalistic "lifeworld" seems quite adequate. Being an agnostic or being indifferent to religion seems to be characteristic of large numbers of persons. It is also true that there are various revivals of religion and various cultist phenomena developing, but modern world culture seems on the whole to be developing into a naturalistic and secular perspective. For many, the apparent peculiarity of God's ontological status is easily explainable because for them, there is no God at all. My point in bringing this up is that the truth of the theistic position is far from obvious. Furthermore, nothing in logic or experience <u>requires</u> that we make this commitment. Even a reasonably coherent social ethics can be developed on a naturalistic basis. The so-called leap of faith is truly a risky leap as far as reason and experience are concerned. It is an odd and peculiar commitment for people to make and we fail to notice how odd it is because of religious cultural conditioning. Christianity makes the oddest and most extreme claim of all--namely, that a personal God loves and cares for each one of us as an individual, as a shepherd does his sheep. Such a claim flies in the face of what experience tells us about humans and their destiny. The Christian may fully recognize this but maintains his faith in spite of it. Others, on the other hand, lose their faith because of it. Ontological commitment to God comes primarily through faith. Ontological commitment to the existence of things and persons comes from presentation in experience. Other types of ontological commitment arise out of theoretical requirements in science and mathematics.

When we compare the two categories of "divinity" and "God" it is apparent that "divinity" is the more defensible because the former category simply marks out certain features of experience that occur phenomenologically. The given value impingement which I have designated by "divinity" can be characterized in a variety of ways. As an example I will suggest that what the later Heidegger calls the disclosure of Being is but one way of describing what I call impingement of divinity. Great caution is needed in making a statement like this. Heidegger is not a religious thinker in the conventional sense of that term. Indeed, he has sometimes been considered an atheist. While there were indications of atheism or agnosticism in his earlier writings, one could scarcely read the later writings and think of him as an atheist. While he is not a theist, one cannot read the later Heidegger without being impressed by his strongly mystical overtones.[3] Indeed, the later works seem to be fraught with religious significance even though the usual religious categories of interpretation do not appear.

This is not the place to get into a detailed discussion of Heidegger's incredibly obscure doctrine of Being--a term that by itself tends to turn off most Anglo-American readers. But the way in which Heidegger talks about Being and about the recovery of Being, about Gelassenheit, about the "letting be" of disclosure, and the whole discussion of dwelling in the fourfold, strongly suggests that Being may be an aspect of what I call phenomenological disclosure of divinity. The gods, of course, appear as one of the fourfold. Earth, sky and mortals are also deeply involved with the gods in the interrelationship of the components of the fourfold. Since Heidegger's concept of dwelling involves the recovery of Being, and dwelling involves the fourfold, it would seem reasonable to see Being (whatever else it might be) as deeply impregnated by divinity. The later Heidegger is marking off certain phenomenological characterizations of experience, some of which I would tend to call aspects of divinity. While it may be appropriate to discuss the later Heidegger in terms of the concept of "divinity," it would clearly be more difficult to talk of his later thought using the concept of "God" and the identification of God and Being would be unjustified.

It is apparent that the concept of "God" is a difficult one to defend philosophically. For one thing, the Being of God is personal in nature and the implausible claim is made that God is lovingly concerned with each one of us individually. It could certainly be the case that all this is so, but the readings of experience do not bear this out in any obvious or clear way.

Once these difficulties are accepted and faced (and they are real difficulties for faith as well as for philosophy) we can go on to talk about various concepts of God. These concepts can be compared with each other on the grounds of both religious adequacy and philosophical coherence. Under these criteria some doctrines of God will be found to be more religiously adequate than others and some will be found to be more philosophically coherent than others. Religious adequacy and philosophical coherence do not necessarily go together, but it is the hope and expectation that an increase in the one will be met by an increase in the other.

By philosophical coherence is meant a doctrine of God that does not embrace inexplicable contradiction and a doctrine which does not go against our deepest findings in experience and science. I find great difficulties in classical theism because it appears to say that God is changeless and immovable, but is also personal and loving. Biblical fundamentalism's doctrine of God is incoherent because the vengeful nature of God violates what we know to be best in persons. Qualities that are applauded in God are condemned when applied to persons. It is incoherent morally, and religiously inadequate for the same reasons. If one is willing to make the faith commitment we can then compare various concepts of God in light of the criteria suggested. When we talk about God, the dyadic character remains, but it is now an ontological rather than phenomenological dyad. If the transition to God is to occur, faith must enter. Philosophy cannot give what faith cannot produce. Given the context of faith, philosophy can help develop concepts of divinity coherent with our experience, moral and otherwise.

The two categories of "divinity" and "God" are useful but distinct. "Divinity" is a category more useful for philosophical explication, while in the west, at any rate, "God" is essential as a religious category in the active life of faith.

NOTES

[1] For further discussion of this point, see Chapter 7.

[2] This may seem an unfair and restrictive statement as far as the tradition is concerned--an expression of a dogmatic empiricism. Nevertheless, I am unpersuaded by the traditional view that sees the universe as requiring God as some kind of ontological principle. I have never been able to see how appealing to God makes the universe or anything else more intelligible than it already is. If there were no empirical grounding of the concept of "God" in divinity, God-talk might be an interesting intellectual enterprise but scarcely the important existential issue for human life which it obviously is.

[3] See John D. Caputo, <u>The Mystical Element in Heidegger's Thought</u> (Athens, OH: Ohio University Press, 1978).

CHAPTER 11

INTIMATIONS AS EPISTEMICALLY USEFUL

> "There are more things in heaven and earth, Horatio, than are dreamt of in your philosophy."
> *Hamlet*, Act I, Scene 5.

While our concern in this book has been with intimations of divinity, there are various kinds of intimations and it may pay us to examine intimations as such, as we come to the conclusion of this study. In addition to intimations of divinity, we have talked about intimations of absurdity and of course Wordsworth is most famous for his "intimations of immortality." As we have seen, intimations arise in experience and involve direct but not immediate givenness of some kind from which extrapolations and interpretations can be made.

For our purposes we have explicated the concept of "intimation" to designate *phenomena* that present themselves in experience, intending that such phenomena not involve one in any kind of ontological commitment. Intimations impinge on consciousness, but such impingement lacks the epistemological justification that one finds in the empirical sciences and in the data of everyday life involving our experience of things and persons.

In resorting to intimations, I not only want to indicate their lack of the usual kinds of epistemic force, but I also wish to avoid a facile reductionism which tends to oversimplify a complex and increasingly mysterious world. While use of intimations clearly involves some speculation, we should keep in mind their phenomenological character recognizing that full blown speculative philosophy naturally and rightly takes you into the realm of explicit ontological commitment involved in metaphysics.

Heidegger, particularly in his later period, is a prime example of intimative speculation carried on at the phenomenological level. What Heidegger calls true "thinking" involves intimations--not intimations of divinity necessarily, though this occurs too, but intimations that are present in human experience but which lack the usually expected epistemic force. A prime example in Heidegger is his attempt to "unpack" the concept of "dwelling," particularly as seen in his discussion of "dwelling in the fourfold."[1] Such intimations are epistemologically useful when we have something particularly important to say about human <u>experience</u>, something that needs uncovering philosophically but that you cannot justify in any ordinarily strong epistemic sense. The power of suggestion is a tool too little used in philosophy and use of this power involves intimations.

To illustrate what I mean I want to apply Heidegger's fruitful concept of "Dwelling" to a specific human experience of the seashore using his distinction of the fourfold--earth, sky, divinities and mortals. In doing this I hope to throw light on what I mean by intimations. Heidegger puts a good deal of weight on his concept of <u>dwelling</u> and before we explicate the shore as dwelling in the fourfold we must first formulate what Heidegger means by _dwelling_. To be a mortal on the earth is to be a temporary resident and one who is aware that he will die in time. One may seek to disguise this fact by retreating into unauthentic modes of being or one may resolutely and authentically live one's life in the realization that one's projects will be terminated in time by death. For Heidegger it is only humans that can live on earth as mortals. In short it is only humans that can dwell, for it is only humans (as far as we know) that possess this kind of consciousness. Animals can perish but it is only human _Dasein_ that can have this kind of "being toward death." Animals (as far as we know) cannot _dwell_ in this sense.

Major features of Heidegger's concept of dwelling are the activities of conserving, building and cultivating. To dwell is to cherish and care for the things that surround one. Ontologically, in Heidegger's sense, mortals dwell by cherishing sky and earth and by gathering them together with awareness of divinities. What Heidegger calls a gathering of the fourfold constitutes dwelling. One does this either by cultivating and cherishing the things of the earth or by building things, constructing them in a manner that gathers the fourfold together. What Heidegger has in mind here is analogous to the manner in which Frank Lloyd Wright builds a house into the rock formations and contours of the surroundings instead of slashing the surroundings away in order to build a house. For Heidegger, dwelling is a basic feature of human beings even though this may be disguised from us in present technological contexts. Although we may build unaware of the full significance of why we build, Heidegger will argue that we build because we are basically dwellers and to dwell is to safeguard each thing in its nature. While our building certainly alters the nature of things, for Heidegger it should do so with minimal violation of the nature of the things that already exist. For example, a cabinet maker builds furniture out of wood, thus altering the shape of things, but as far as possible he preserves and enhances the nature of the wood rather than violating it altogether in terms of some preconceived design.

Let us explicate Heidegger's concept of dwelling further by applying it to my example of the seashore and follow this up by talking about the fourfold in terms of the shore example. When we speak of dwelling, we are speaking of specific places where a gathering together of the fourfold occurs. Heidegger's example is of a bridge across a river or a stream which designates a specific location. Dwelling, thus, refers us to a specific place; when I speak of the shore I am thinking of a particular place to which I have gone for years. Like any other location, my seashore place occupies a geographical area and has a history behind it. It can be spoken of in political, sociological and biological terms, but its dwelling character resides in the fact that mortals (humans) have given the place a special significance in terms of the <u>interest in it</u> and in terms of their <u>response to it</u>.

It became a dwelling place when people erected hotels and cottages and built the fishing pier and boardwalk. It is the building of these structures that gives it location in Heidegger's sense. The interest of humans in the place, of course, derived from their response to it when they first encountered it (primarily in the modes of earth and sky) as we shall indicate later. This particular shore place is a dwelling in that humans built in a way which did not destroy the surroundings but preserved and cared for what was already there, because what was already there in terms of earth and sky was what originally drew people to this place. It is also a dwelling in that persons and their families have returned there year after year from one generation to the next. Cottages were built so that the dunes were preserved, though in recent years there has been further and further dune encroachment, but there still remains interest in dune preservation and measures have been taken to insure that what is left remains. The boardwalk is not an encroachment on the beach, but sits so that it enhances and does not detract from the whole panorama of beach and sea. To sense the opposite of the shore as dwelling one has only to think of places like Atlantic City where people come and go and where boardwalk and casinos dominate the shore rather than gather the shore together sharing human concerns with the needs of the larger environment.

There are always dangers that purely commercial interests will eventually destroy my "place" at the shore as a dwelling.

A place can be a vacation spot and a place to live without being a dwelling. But so far, except for minor encroachments my place at the shore remains a dwelling in Heidegger's sense. It is where people have built in the mode of gathering together of the fourfold--where mortals have drawn together earth, sky and divinities. We shall have to look at what this might mean in terms of intimations about my particular place at the shore.

The basic aspects of the fourfold are set forth by Heidegger in the following fashion:

> Earth is the serving bearer, blossoming and fruiting, spreading out in rock and water, rising up into plant and animal. When we say earth, we are already thinking of the other three along with it, but we give no thought to the simple oneness of the four.
>
> The sky is the vaulting path of the sun, the course of the changing moon, the wandering glitter of the stars, the year's seasons and their changes, the light and dusk of day, the gloom and glow of night, the clemency and inclemency of the weather, the drifting clouds and blue depth of the ether. When we say sky, we are already thinking of the other three along with it, but we give no thought to the simple oneness of the four.
>
> The divinities are the beckoning messengers of the godhead. Out of the holy sway of the godhead, the god appears in his presence or withdraws into his concealment. When we speak of the divinities, we are already thinking of the other three along with them, but we give no thought to the simple oneness of the four.
>
> The mortals are the human beings. They are called mortals because they can die. To die means to be capable of death <u>as</u> death. Only man dies, and indeed continually, as long as he remains on earth, under the sky, before

> the divinities. When we speak of mortals, we are already thinking of the other three along with them, but we give no thought to the simple oneness of the four.[2]

The simple oneness of the four Heidegger calls the fourfold, and mortals dwell in the way they preserve the fourfold. All of this sounds mystical and obscure, particularly to philosophers steeped in the analytic tradition but I want to give a phenomenological explication of what is involved using my example of a seashore residence which is specific, vivid and concrete. This will also give a clearer and concrete example of intimations in general.

In ordinary terms we speak of the seashore location as a recreational resource, and/or a wildlife refuge resource--we see it in what Heidegger calls the technological mode of "standing reserve."[3] That is, we see it as a place to go on vacation, as a source of relaxation, as a place to get away from it all. As vacationland, the shore is more or less seen in the mode of what Heidegger calls equipment--it is used and adapted to our ends and purposes. This view is particularly apparent in real estate and Chamber of Commerce brochures that are sent to encourage people to come. When we are there on vacation, we spend most of our time walking the beach, swimming, sunbathing, boating, fishing, eating or whatever else we do to have a good time. Some spend most of their time gambling, drinking or playing cards and in such contexts the shore is simply an incidental background to such activities. To those who spend most of their time on the beach or on the water, the shore is more than an incidental background. It is essential to the human activity of having a vacation. Nevertheless, we are still speaking of the seashore primarily as a tool of, or resource for, human recreational activities.

The shore seen as resource or "standing reserve" is even more apparent when viewed from the perspective of the real estate agent, the restaurant owner, the lifeguard or the police. These are the producing agents who spend their time seeing to it that the consumers have a good time, that their vacations are worthwhile, and enticing them to return again. The real estate agent may enjoy the shore as a consumer briefly when the season is over but, for the most part, his activities are centered around real estate development. For the summer college student, lifeguard or waitress there are elements of both vacation and work but, in either capacity, the seashore is experienced mainly in the mode of "standing reserve"--e.g., as a source of summer income and as a chance for romantic encounter, learning how to surfboard or picking up a good tan. While drudgery may be involved in experiencing the shore in the mode of "standing reserve," one should not assume that a great deal of enjoyment is not also involved. After all, most of these vacationing activities are fun and even the work aspects may be enjoyable as well. These are our usual ways of experiencing the world, using the seashore as an example. In our activities the world is something to be used, absorbed and reacted to. To us this is intelligible, natural and understandable. What becomes cloudy and obscure is

Heidegger's talk about the fourfold and the modes of experience involved.

Heidegger's contention is that the fourfold is essential to healthy human "dwelling" and that the West has lost an awareness of what it is to "dwell." We are very good at the technological mode of seeing the world as "standing reserve," but exclusive reliance on this mode entails what Heidegger calls a "loss of "Being." There is nothing intrinsically wrong with viewing the world as "standing reserve"--indeed it is essential to modern life to do so, but if we are to recover our spiritual well-being we must be open to the fourfold as a road towards the "recovering of Being."

THE SEASHORE AS EARTH

What we will be talking about throughout are ways supplementary to seeing the shore as "standing reserve," not substitutions for seeing it in this way. We will be talking about my Intimations of the Shore. Experience of earth in this sense is the feeling of being a part of the earth, as being rooted to the earth and drawing sustenance from it. More is involved than being intellectually aware that we are dependent on the earth or possessing ecological knowledge of "spaceship earth"; the shore as earth is a more primordial feeling of our "rootedness" in the earth, our springing from it and our return to it. The immensity of the ocean, the extensive length of the beach, the endless grains of sand, the flight of the birds as they come home to roost at dusk in the bird sanctuary, the sharp smell of a sea breeze, the fog or mist rolling across the ocean and the beach, the disturbed slightly threatening quality of the gray ocean waves on a stormy day or the appearance of dolphins in the green-blue water on a clear day--all of these experiences may enhance our feeling of the seashore as earth.

Walk on the beach alone sometime during a strong rain and windstorm when nobody else is around, when the waves are rough and when the rain hits you horizontally. It may not be very pleasant, let alone be what you are paying to experience at the shore--but it is the seashore as earth. In many ways it is easier to experience the shore as earth in off-season than when it is crowded with people, but it is not essential to do so--the shore as earth is simply more apparent at these times--it discloses itself more easily in the off-season contexts--but it can be disclosed as earth at any time. Earth is also the heightened significance of particular places in Heidegger's sense of "dwelling." Heidegger's own example is of a bridge across the Rhine at a particular place. In my example I am not thinking of the seashore in general, but of a particular place--of particular items on the beach like the fishing pier extending out into the water, the location of the old theatre on the boardwalk, various locations on the boardwalk itself and the groin of rocks at the inlet where the tides shift the sands from year to year. Each place is replete with vivid memories.

<u>Place</u>, for Heidegger, is not just a geographical location on a map but a gathering together of human concerns and

interests where earth, sky and gods are disclosed to mortals. One's home may be the most obvious example of place in Heidegger's sense. By "earth" Heidegger is talking about a particular phenomenological way of "being in the world"--a particular aspect of world disclosure. The seashore as earth may be casually noticed or also appear in the context of some human project to be accomplished. The inlet is a place to walk to, the pier is a place to fish from, but these are places that can also be simply apprehended for what they are--with no pragmatic concerns in mind--one can be open to the disclosure of them, for the enhancement of one's experience. I do not mean to imply that experience of the shore as earth is necessarily rare or particularly esoteric. It would seem quite possible that one might simultaneously experience the world in terms of everyday human projects and experience it as earth at the same time. I have the suspicion that many fishermen, sitting quietly for hours at a time, experience the shore as earth, but in our culture it helps to be engaged in a project too. One may enjoy fishing as a goal or one may fish for money, but one looks like a damn fool if one just sits and gazes at the ocean for any length of time, without some human project being undertaken too.

For Heidegger, the earth discloses itself as the place where mortals dwell and the seashore discloses itself to us as earth when we pay attention to it, either by immersing ourselves in its wonders deliberately or in the midst of pragmatic everyday activities. The disclosure of earth is more obvious in dramatic natural scenery but its disclosure is not impossible in routine settings. The disclosure of seashore as earth requires a special <u>paying attention</u>, more or less in the aesthetic mode of receptivity. In short, disclosure of the seashore as earth is phenomenologically a different way of being at the seashore than viewing it <u>only</u> in terms of one's projects and interests.

Since apprehension of the shore as earth is a special way of experiencing, it may help to clarify the matter by relating it to environmental issues. Contemporary concerns with the environment have a twofold focus. One is a pragmatic concern with preserving the environment as a suitable habitation for humans. This focus attempts intellectually to raise our consciousness concerning the dire consequences to humans when we fail to be concerned with environmental issues. Environment is dealt with in the technological mode and is primarily a conceptual intellectual enterprise extending human knowledge in these areas. The other focus is <u>feeling</u> emotionally about environmental issues in experiencing the world as earth. Actually a good many environmentalists approach the issue on both levels, but much of the passionate motivation that goes into environmental issues comes from people who strongly apprehend the world as earth.

Concern with the environment of the shore as earth consists in much more than viewing it <u>only</u> in terms of how we can preserve and enhance human life. To experience the shore as earth is to feel that in the last analysis we share it with the gulls and the sandpipers. It is to feel that we are integrally a part of the animal and plant life of the shore and to feel that to some degree, other creatures than humans should be accorded some basic rights of survival. Admittedly these rights are not absolute and one has to fit them into the context of human concerns, but to view the shore as earth is to view it as something more than only a means to satisfy human needs, important as that is. Much of the philosophical thrust of environmentalism consists in seeing the world as earth in Heidegger's sense. The emotive fervor behind much of the movement comes from this perspective and is an ontic expression of viewing the world as earth. The fourfold can serve as philosophical underpinning for much environmentalism and though most would be unaware of this, Heidegger is the philosophic voice that most vigorously expresses these concerns. Heidegger, to be sure, remains, for the most part, on the ontological level--he was not writing an ethic, a philosophy of religion or a philosophical explanation of environmentalism, but at the ontic level it is plausible to see much environmental fervor as an expression of seeing the shore as earth. To see the shore as earth is to see it as having intrinsic worth and value in itself in addition to the value that it has for human beings.

THE SEASHORE AS SKY

Here we are talking about the seashore and our awareness of it in the shifting patterns of daylight, dusk, night and early morning. As in the case of earth, a receptive awareness is called for. Sunrise over the ocean is qualitatively quite distinct from sunset over the ocean. The space and sky in which the shore is experienced are quite different during the bright light of day and after dusk--after the sun has set and before it gets completely dark. Photographers are aware of how much more vivid things appear in early morning or late afternoon in their sharpness as compared to the somewhat more "flattened out" impressions that one has at midday. Under the aspect of sky, Heidegger includes changes of weather and changes of season. I have already spoken of weather changes under the shore as earth, but for Heidegger this would probably fall under the shore as sky. The repetition of the changing seasons would be crucial under the shore as sky. Each of the four seasons has its own textural properties and disclosure occurs dramatically in each. There is a cold barrenness about winter at the shore. More days are apt to be stormy; the beaches are empty of people except for occasional wanderers and at my shore most of the houses are empty, the market is closed and the town takes on rather a spooky appearance even at midday. But spring will arrive, a few more houses and motels will begin to open and real estate activity will intensify. The cold of the beach will begin to diminish as the days lengthen. The pragmatic everyday activities of the summer season change the felt character of the beach in crucial and not always desirable ways. In early morning, the noisy equipment arrives to rake the beach on behalf of the intent vacationers. Lifeguard stands appear and whistles blow to keep bathers and surfers in assigned areas. The cries of children at play, annoyed parents, and an ocean filled with catamarans and windsurfers is a recurring seasonal feature that must be a wonder and disturbance to the gulls and sandpipers which generally have the beach to themselves. After Labor Day the gulls and sandpipers begin to regain possession of the beach--the vacationers begin to fade away slowly, the whistling lifeguards are gone, the beach no longer is raked and quietness begins to take over for the long stillness of winter. When we speak of the seashore as sky, it is the more or less invariable and repetitious nature and passage of the seasons that Heidegger seems to have in mind.

The phenomenological apprehension of the shore as earth and sky are closely interrelated without any clear sharp dividing line between them. Of course, the fourfold are not really divided for Heidegger and are all to be apprehended as one, but it seems that there is a sense in which earth and sky go together in a way which is not as apparent when we think of divinities and mortals. Under the modes of earth and sky, the shore discloses itself in all its aesthetic richness in that it presents itself simply as a panorama to be experienced and enjoyed. Heidegger's concern is that with our exclusive preoccupation with the world as "standing reserve," modern man has lost his openness to these more primal modes of disclosure. As we saw earlier, even a vacation is often pursued with a businesslike intensity. If one spends most of one's time viewing the world as "standing reserve" in terms of resources to be used, it is very hard to break this pattern on a two week vacation; thus, the shore gets viewed in this mode too and most of its elusive enchantment goes unnoticed. Heidegger is not arguing that we should give up seeing the world in technological terms, but it is no accident that our ecological despoliation is due in large part to our failure to apprehend the world in any other mode. Nevertheless, the argument is not being made that one should apprehend the world exclusively as earth and sky, for then nothing would be accomplished or be done.

Now we reach a subject that is difficult to deal with and less persuasive, at least to modern consciousness. Divinities are peculiar to those of us raised in the monotheistically oriented west. Before we talk about application of divinities to the shore we must say something more about this particular aspect of the fourfold. My suspicion is that Heidegger's talk of divinities is an attempt to deal with the religious dimension of experience in more or less neutral terms as far as different cultures are concerned. While he is talking mainly in terms of the monotheistic west, Heidegger's discussion of the presence and withdrawal of the gods in experience is a phenomenon present in any culture. Heidegger speaks of the god as appearing in his presence and withdrawing into his concealment.[4]

Leaving the metaphysical issue of God aside, what Heidegger is saying is that a sense of divine presence is sharper in some cultures than in others and that in a given culture, the sense of divine presence waxes and wanes as the culture develops. What particularly concerns Heidegger is the present spiritual state of western culture. He extends Nietzsche's view that phenomenologically, "God is dead." Since the west is dominated by technological norms there remains very little real sense of the presence of God as a factor in human decision making. Thus, for Heidegger the divinities have withdrawn--the gods have fled. Such withdrawal may be temporary and the reappearance may take radically new forms, but, for the present, a sense of the presence of the divine is not a marked feature of the cultural experience of vast numbers of us.

One may wonder whether the withdrawal of the gods is the cause of our technologically based hedonistic culture or whether the technologically oriented culture is the cause of the withdrawal of the gods--perhaps the causality works both ways. In any case, if one lives in the world in *exclusively* technological terms, it is not surprising that our sense of divine presence is considerably diminished, if not absent altogether. Heidegger's formulation of the issue is less extreme and somewhat more hopeful, from a religious viewpoint, than Nietzsche's. The latter said, "God is dead." Heidegger's intimation is that "the gods have withdrawn." The divine dimension in experience is submerged, dormant, but it could reemerge again, possibly in a quite different form.

With his prime emphasis on truth as disclosure, it would seem that Heidegger believes there is a divine dimension to human experience and that the "recovery of the sense of Being" would be the reawakening of this aspect. Indeed, the divine is a crucial aspect of the fourfold. I am aware of the danger of identifying God with Being in the philosophy of Heidegger. The temptation to make a theologian of him must be resisted, but the mystical overtones of his later thought plus his explicit reference to divinities as part of the fourfold make it plausible to argue that there is a religious or divine dimension to Heidegger's account of experience. While resisting the temptation of seeing Heidegger in theological terms, one cannot read the later Heidegger without realizing that we are dealing with something that goes beyond a purely naturalistic or humanistic standpoint. What this element is continues to be debated by Heidegger scholars.

Experiencing the phenomenological aspect of divinity is rarer than experiencing the world as earth or sky. Such experiences can occur along with our experiences of earth and sky and also can be taken as disclosure of divinity. One might argue at this point that such disclosure is really only interpretation put upon our awareness of earth and sky by people who are religiously inclined to do so, and is, thus, not really disclosure at all, even phenomenologically. Undoubtedly, this frequently occurs--but, as we have seen, there seems to be disclosure of the divine as there is of earth and sky, only rarer. Of course it should be clear that for Heidegger, earth and sky are not purely physical--there is an overlay of the mystical and the numinous and since the fourfold is ultimately one, divinity is disclosed in earth and sky too, though most of us would not be aware of it. As we saw earlier, disclosure of the divine seems to involve disclosure of aspects of the world also, as seen in a special way, and not disclosure of the divine _alone_. It is interesting that Heidegger too speaks of _intimations_ of divinities.[5]

THE SHORE AS DISCLOSURE OF THE DIVINITIES

Now let us turn to our shore example again. If you go back to the specific examples I gave of disclosure of the shore as earth and sky, one can say that for _some_, these disclosures are also taken as intimations or disclosures of the divine in experience, not as _inferences_ to the divine. Such experiences would, in short, be taken as mystical experiences and be received in a worshipful and reverent context. It is obvious that one could experience the shore as earth and sky without taking such experiences as divine disclosure as well, although Heidegger would want to contend that divinity is embedded in such experiences but would be concealed from consciousness. Anyone familiar with Heidegger is aware of how important the concepts of concealment and unconcealment are in his philosophy. While it is obvious that in one sense one could take experiences of earth and sky on one's own terms without taking them as disclosure of divinity, still when Heidegger talks about earth and sky there is a poetic and religious overtone in his language--a vaguely numinous quality hangs over these experiences as he described them which seems to be absent from descriptions of our experiences in the pragmatic mode of "standing reserve." One should be hesitant in saying that intimations of divinity could not occur in pragmatic contexts--indeed I think they can occur--but the potential unconcealedness of the divine in experience of earth and sky is more apparent.

When we come to our experience of the shore itself, the joy of experiencing the immensity of sky, water and beach, and the healing qualities of such experiences, these can make us _feelingly aware_ that we are a part of a larger scheme of things that makes sense and is good. Again I am not talking about _drawing an inference_ that such is the case. To be feelingly aware is to identify a peculiar _texture_ of experience that may be phenomenologically present in the experience. The inference would be highly risky and subject to much dispute--the awareness need be only noted and marked as part of the Heideggerian fourfold as phenomenally presented. The predominant _texture_ of experiencing the seashore as a disclosure of the divinities is that the seashore itself induces the feeling that one is protected in some peculiar sense--that the shore is part of me and I am part of it and that what is most valuable in human life is somehow conserved. No better characterization of such experience is given than that by James in his _The Varieties of Religious Experience_:

> Summing up in the broadest possible way the characteristics of religious life, as we have found them, it includes the following beliefs:
>
> 1. That the visible world is part of a

> more spiritual universe from which it draws its chief significance;
>
> 2. That union or harmonious relation with that higher universe is our true end;
>
> 3. That prayer or inner communion with the spirit thereof--be that spirit "God" or "law"--is a process wherein work is really done, and spiritual energy flows in and produces effects, psychological or material, within the phenomenal world.
>
> Religion also includes the following psychological characteristics:
>
> 4. A new zest which adds itself like a gift to life, and takes the form either of lyrical enchantment or of appeal to earnestness and heroism.
>
> 5. An assurance of safety and a temper of peace, and, in relation to others, a preponderance of loving affections.[6]

James refers to religious <u>beliefs</u>, but one might more accurately speak of the given <u>textures</u> of our religious experience and I think this is what James really intends. This is not to deny that beliefs may accompany this feeling, but let us keep the beliefs distinct from the experiences that generate them. It would be quite natural for the experience to generate such beliefs but one can simply accept the experience on its own terms without constructing a religious belief system. Taking disclosure of the shore as earth and sky to be disclosure of divinities as well might be illustrated as follows. The feeling of the sublime immensity of the ocean or the extensive expanse of beach might be supplemented by a feeling that all of this and I myself are part of a larger spiritual context that is valuable and life-enhancing, not only to me but to others as well. My experience of the shore may give me a new zest for life combined with the feeling that my projects are not only important to me but make some kind of sense in the larger scheme of things. Much of this life enhancement is a simple result of recreation which one would expect a shore vacation to provide. Recreation means to "re-create" oneself enabling one to reenter the workaday world refreshed and this could occur without bringing in any references to divinities at all. To take such shore experiences as disclosure of the divinities as well, one would have to feel that such experiences were impregnated with religious significance. A sense of the presence of divinities would have to pervade the whole texture of such experiences. While such experiences may not be usual or fantastically widespread, they are by no means rare oddities and if one pays heed to mystical literature such experiences do occur.

Heidegger speaks again and again of experience as unveiling and disclosing various things, or of veiling or hiding them. It is characteristic of our times that in terms of experience, the divinities are veiled or hidden--thus, this becomes the most problematic of the fourfold for modern man to deal with. If such disclosure occurs it is because such experiences are taken to be disclosures of the divine as well. Thus, we have three of the fourfold and must now turn and consider the last.

THE SHORE FOR MORTALS

Heidegger characterizes mortals as those beings capable

of death as death and by this he means human beings. All things in the world perish sooner or later but Heidegger wants to reserve the term death for humans alone--they are the only beings capable of death as death. We need not get into an involved discussion of <u>Dasein</u> and its being towards death in Heidegger's writings--suffice it to say it is humans alone (as far as we know) who can anticipate their own deaths. It is humans alone (as far as we know) who can be consciously aware that all of their projects will end in death. It is true that death can be approached authentically or unauthentically, but either way it is humans who act authentically or unauthentically. For Heidegger only humans (mortals) die--all other creatures simply perish. Thus, the last of the fourfold are mortals--the creatures who die and who can apprehend what it means to live towards death.

The shore as sky makes us conscious of the passages of the seasons. Fall and winter follow spring and summer and beach season follows beach season and I know that at some time these seasonal changes will end abruptly for me, but they will continue for others. I am older now than I was. I recall experiencing the beach as a child of six and being terrified of the sand blowing against my legs in a storm. I have experienced the same blowing sand many times since but now without the terror, and I know that there will come a time when I will experience it no more. The same beach that I romped over joyously as a child, God willing, I will hobble over sometime with a cane. As a mortal I also note the passage of time in my place at the shore. I remember how the boardwalk was <u>then</u> and how it is now--the inlet seemed miles away <u>then</u>, but only a short distance <u>now</u>. I note the passing away of train service, the increasing number of houses and the increasing diminishment of the tall dunes as human habitation spreads further and further. I recall, however, with joy the same smells and sounds of the sea that I experienced years ago. As a mortal I know that my father can no longer drive me around while I sit on the front fender of the car on a summer evening and I know that there will be a time when I will be gone, my projects brought to an end. Other children and adults will laugh and breathe in the shore with joy. We are mortals and amidst the joy of experiencing the shore a sudden pang occurs, for these experiences are transitory and will pass and I as mortal know this.

Thus, the fourfold of the shore is complete and if you look back at the quotations from Heidegger you will see that the fourfold is a oneness. He says of each of them that we give no thought to the simple oneness of the four. Thus, Heidegger uses the fourfold to explicate his concept of "dwelling." We live in houses and work at our projects and activities of everyday life. We live in Philadelphia, Birmingham and Atlanta; we are <u>in</u> textiles, housing and the restaurant business, but for Heidegger, most of us have forgotten how to "dwell." It is not a question of living or dwelling, but of doing both. Until we learn to do both, we shall continue to live in a state of alienation from ourselves, from those around us and from the world. I picked the example of the shore because it is a very special case for me and has been over the years and I suspect that this is because, in Heidegger's terms, it is a dwelling place for me. I like to go to the seashore in various places around the world, but only this place is for me a dwelling in the full sense of the word. In the context of "standing reserve" it is like many other places at the shore here and abroad. As "standing reserve" one shore place will more or less be as good as another, but as _dwelling_, only this place will do. A hometown is or was, for many, a dwelling. As "standing reserve" it may lack many resources, but for me it is home. It should be pointed out that a place could _come to be_ a dwelling for someone--it would not have to be a place one knew as a child or grew up in. Also, more than one place could be a dwelling in Heidegger's sense. What is required for it as a dwelling is that it be experienced in the mode of the fourfold, possibly not as fully as Heidegger insists, but at least crucial features of the fourfold would be present. Dwelling is a gathering of the fourfold together. A place that is not a dwelling is simply a place where one lives, works or visits--a place more or less interchangeable with similar places. Thus, we have explicated the seashore as dwelling. It is to the recovery of our sense of dwelling that Heidegger directs us and his thought is a fruitful guidepost for further exploration.

My treatment of the seashore is also intended to

illustrate, by specific example, intimation in general using Heidegger's fourfold. Leaving divinity aside, it is apparent that earth, sky and mortals have straightforward empirical uses that can be spoken of in the usual strong epistemic terms. It is also clear that Heidegger is not using these terms in their ordinary senses. Yet as I hope my example has shown, talk of the fourfold is meant to strongly <u>suggest</u> important features of experience which occur frequently but which lack strong epistemic force. It may be a fruitful task to talk about Heideggerian "thinking" in terms of phenomenological intimations and vice versa. Much fruitful work remains to be done in this area.

Given my example of the seashore one might ask what <u>intimations</u> are involved in the use of the fourfold? As was the case earlier with Peirce, I will <u>use</u> Heidegger's phenomenological concept here to explicate further the idea of intimation I have been developing in this study, hoping to remain within the spirit of Heidegger's enterprise but not primarily attempting to explain him. In the case of the seashore, earth, sky and mortals make their appearance in addition to the gods. Unlike the gods, earth, sky and mortals can be designated in straightforward empirical ways. As straightforward empirical concepts they have the usual epistemic force of concepts that have a public use and acceptance.

However, as appearing in Heidegger's doctrine of the fourfold, earth, sky, mortals and gods are developed in terms of Heidegger's obscure concept of "dwelling." The use of the term "mortals" is the one closest of the four to ordinary empirical usage. Empirically, we all die sooner or later and this we share in common with all animals and plants. But this "fact" is not what is of primary interest in usage of the term "mortal" in the fourfold. What is of interest here is the realization on the part of myself that I will die eventually and that the shore place of my dwelling will continue in some form or other--either to be a dwelling to others or else be destroyed as a dwelling by technology. I _feel_ my own mortality when I reflect on this, and this is what differentiates me from animals and plants which simply perish and as far as I know do not have this awareness. One might respond that we are still within the ordinary empirical realm--everybody feels their own mortality from time to time and it is quite obvious I will die and that this belief is epistemically justifiable in ordinary ways. But Heidegger wants to go further, maintaining that Dasein is involved in Being towards death. Ontologically my being is a selfhood projected towards _my_ death as an awareness that _my_ death will be the end of all _my_ projects, and this is different from the simple empirical truth that "all men are mortal." For me this means ontically that I have poignant awareness that the seashore place I love will not miss me when I am gone--the life of the beach, and the activity of the windsurfers and the fishing from the pier will go on as before. All of this still seems straightforward and empirical. Why invoke _intimations_ of mortality in talking about mortals in the fourfold? Intimations suggest what I would call textures of experience which characterize my being in the world. Call them textures, signals, intimations, "raw feels," they characterize my experience but are generally not obvious or public enough to justify beliefs in the strong epistemic sense of everyday life and science. Suppose for a moment that I did not know the empirical truth that "all men are mortal." I think it fair to say that even in this case I would have intimations of my own forthcoming mortality--intimations that I could not justify in ordinary empirical ways. Of course, I also know that all men are mortal, but this knowledge is different from the lonely sense that the beach and shore will go on long after I am gone. Intimations are manifested in twinges of regret and loss which occur when I become aware of the passage of time and the limited amount of time left to me. This is the intimation of mortality in the fourfold. In this case it happens that I also have hard knowledge that I will die in a finite time, but this is not the same as Heideggerian mortality. As we have seen I also have intimations of divinity and I may also have intimations of immortality as well. Since I have hard evidence that I will die, at least bodily, it would be contradictory to say that I have hard evidence that I am immortal. But I can and do have contradictory intimations or at least intimations that seem to conflict with each other, but since the epistemic force is so weak, I am not forced to choose. We have already seen that we have intimations of cosmic absurdity as well as of divinity. In a similar way I have intimations of my own mortality as well as intimations of some kind of survival of my bodily death. The law of contradiction does not seem to reign in the area of intimations.

The intimative character of Heideggerian earth and sky is even more apparent than is mortality. In addition to the ordinary empirical manifestations of earth and sky, appearance in the fourfold discloses the textures of experience in general and the textures of my experience of the shore in these modes in particular as we have already seen. The ontic analysis of earth and sky at the seashore intimates and discloses significant aspects of human experience. This has been described already in this chapter and enough has been said about divinity in other parts of this study. Ontologically the textures of Dasein's being in the world are well indicated by dwelling in the fourfold and are illustrated ontically by my example of the seashore.

Intimations of various kinds represent a phenomenological "database" from which metaphysical speculation can proceed if one chooses to go this route. Various intimations are also embedded in a larger phenomenological epistemically more secure "database" of ordinary experiences. Not enough attention has been paid to intimations even at the phenomenological level. Hopefully this study will help to rectify this imbalance, at least in the area of philosophy of religion.

NOTES

[1] Martin Heidegger, "Building, Dwelling, Thinking" in Poetry, Language, Thought, trans. Albert Hofstader (New York: Harper, 1971) pp. 149-151.

[2] Ibid, pp. 149-150.

[3] Martin Heidegger, The Question Concerning Technology, trans. William Lovitt (New York: Harper, 1977) p. 17.

[4] "Building, Dwelling, Thinking," p. 150.

[5] Ibid.

[6] William James, The Varieties of Religious Experience (New York: Longmans, Green and Co., 1935) pp. 485-486.

CONCLUSION

As a result of this study the following conclusions seem appropriate. Two types of readers will be unhappy about the ambiguities apparent in the study and the failure to draw strong conclusions from one perspective or another. The people of firm religious faith will desire something far more positive and direct than simply intimations of divinity, and the tough-minded naturalists will be impatient with my "fiddling around" with vague intimations of divinity and will opt for a strong empistemological naturalism, devoid of the ambiguities presented by religious experience.

My response is that all experience is fraught with ambiguity, not just religious experience. Experience presents many faces to us providing room for multiple interpretations. Coupled with the rejection of foundationalism by most schools of contemporary philosophy, the ambiguous character of experience will come as no surprise to many believers and to many tough-minded empiricists. Still those strongly committed to one approach or the other will feel my conclusions are inadequate.

In the eyes of faith, doubt will seem to many to be a betrayal of the religious consciousness. For many, faith, to be strong, must repress doubt. This attitude, to be sure, is found more in the general public than in the philosophically aware believer. For the latter, faith can live with the tension of doubt, and indeed one might push further and argue that dynamic faith needs the tension of doubt to be healthy and active. It is certainly one of the main contentions of this study that any religious faith worthy of belief must face and accept the full dimensions of evil that are apparent and recognize the cogency of the intimations of absurdity while willingly making a faith commitment that goes beyond the intimations of divinity.

In the eyes of tough-minded naturalism religious faith is not only a blind repression of doubt, but a childish wish fantasy seeking to escape from facing the real problems of a perplexing world. As James remarked in his response to W. K. Clifford,[1] the naturalist refuses to be duped by hope and thus fears to make any commitments beyond hard evidence. James himself, while admitting the absence of hard evidence, would prefer to be duped by hope for man's future rather than be imprisoned by a fear of going beyond the evidence. The only response I would make to a tough-minded naturalism at this point is not to close options by defining experience too narrowly or by confining epistemological investigations to conventional and obvious contexts. The world is a far stranger place than any of us have any idea of, as physicists and biologists keep reminding us.

As for any philosophy that calls itself empiricist, it should remain open to all the ambiguities of experience. To be open to the multifaceted world of experience is to be duped by neither fear nor hope. Whatever my own commitments or my readers' commitments may be, we should realize that there are bound to be important experiences which could count against such commitments. Does that mean faith commitments should not be made? No. Such commitments, however, should be made and held with "fear and trembling," with full awareness of the ambiguities involved. While our reading of experience may be wrong, it is also conceivable that you or I may come "close to the mark." Of course, as far as this life is concerned neither one of us will ever know what "the mark" is because to have such knowledge would be to have a god's eye view of <u>all that is</u> and this we have seen is impossible.

In this "crazy quilt world," intimations of divinity are worth developing and pursuing in the face of absurdity and evil. Indeed, there is hardly anything more worth pursuing if humans are to make sense of their world and live at peace with one another. If it were not for the importance of such "gut level" "raw feels," I should not have deemed it worthwhile to expend the efforts that I have on this study. I often feel that the search for the disclosure of divinity is something like the radio astronomer listening for intelligent signals from outer space. There is a lot of ground clutter and static to clear away. Happily, the signals of transcendence are stronger than the as yet non-existent, intelligent radio signals from outer space. Divinity and God may once again return in fuller force to human consciousness.

NOTES

[1] William James, "The Will to Believe" in *Essays in Pragmatism* (New York: Hafner Publishing Company, 1949) pp.88-110.

BIBLIOGRAPHY

Berger, Peter L. A Rumor of Angels. Garden City, NY: Doubleday Anchor, 1970.

Bollnow, Otto Friedrich. "The Conquest of Existentialism." Universitas. Vol. 2, No. 2, 1958.

Caputo, John D. The Mystical Element in Heidegger's Thought. Athens, OH: Ohio University Press, 1978.

Findlay, J. N. The Discipline of the Cave. London, George Allen and Unwin, 1966.

Hartshorne, Charles. Man's Vision of God. Hamden, CT: Archon Books, 1964.

-------------------. The Divine Relativity. New Haven: Yale University Press, 1948.

-------------------. The Logic of Perfection and Other Essays in Neoclassical Metaphysics. La Salle, IL: Open Court, 1962.

Hartshorne, Charles and Reese, Willam. Philosophers Speak of God. Chicago: University of Chicago Press, 1953.

Hartshorne, Charles and Weiss, Paul, eds. Collected Papers of Charles Sanders Peirce. 8 Vols. Cambridge, MA: Harvard University Press, 1960.

Heidegger, Martin. Poetry, Language, Thought. Trans. Albert Hofstader. New York: Harper, 1971.

-----------------. The Question Concerning Technology. Trans. William Lovitt. New York: Harper, 1977.

Hume, David. "Dialogues Concerning Natural Religion." The

English Philosophers from Bacon to Mill. Ed. E. A. Burtt. New York: Random House, 1939.

James, William. Essays in Pragmatism. New York: Hafner Publishing Co., 1948.

--------------. The Varieties of Religious Experience. New York: Longmans, Green and Co., 1935.

Kant, Immanuel. Critique of Pure Reason. Trans. Norman Kemp Smith. New York: The Macmillan Co., 1929.

Lewis, C. I. An Analysis of Knowledge and Valuation. La Salle, IL: Open Court, 1946.

Otto, Rudolf. The Idea of the Holy. New York: Galaxy Books, 1958.

Smith, John. Experience and God. New York: Oxford University Press, 1968.

Unamuno, Miguel De. The Tragic Sense of Life. New York: Dover Publications, 1954.

Whitehead, A. N. Religion in the Making. New York: Meridian, 1960.

---------------. Science and the Modern World. New York: Mentor Books, 1963.

DATE DUE